MW00490790

About Island Press

Since 1984, the nonprofit organization Island Press has been stimulating, shaping, and communicating ideas that are essential for solving environmental problems worldwide. With more than 800 titles in print and some 40 new releases each year, we are the nation's leading publisher on environmental issues. We identify innovative thinkers and emerging trends in the environmental field. We work with world-renowned experts and authors to develop cross-disciplinary solutions to environmental challenges.

Island Press designs and executes educational campaigns in conjunction with our authors to communicate their critical messages in print, in person, and online using the latest technologies, innovative programs, and the media. Our goal is to reach targeted audiences—scientists, policymakers, environmental advocates, urban planners, the media, and concerned citizens—with information that can be used to create the framework for long-term ecological health and human well-being.

Island Press gratefully acknowledges major support of our work by The Agua Fund, The Andrew W. Mellon Foundation, Betsy & Jesse Fink Foundation, The Bobolink Foundation, The Curtis and Edith Munson Foundation, Forrest C. and Frances H. Lattner Foundation, G.O. Forward Fund of the Saint Paul Foundation, Gordon and Betty Moore Foundation, The Kresge Foundation, The Margaret A. Cargill Foundation, New Mexico Water Initiative, a project of Hanuman Foundation, The Overbrook Foundation, The S.D. Bechtel, Jr. Foundation, The Summit Charitable Foundation, Inc., V. Kann Rasmussen Foundation, The Wallace Alexander Gerbode Foundation, and other generous supporters.

The opinions expressed in this book are those of the author(s) and do not necessarily reflect the views of our supporters.

URBAN
ACUPUNCTURE

URBAN
ACUPUNCTURE

Jaime Lerner

Washington | Covelo | London

Translated from the Portuguese by Mac Margolis, Peter Muello, and Ariadne Daher.

K⊢ Knight Foundation

This project was made possible with the support
of the John S. and James L. Knight Foundation.

Island Press would also like to acknowledge the collaboration
of the Center for the Living City.

Library of Congress Control Number: 2014944763

Printed on recycled, acid-free paper ♲

Manufactured in the United States of America
10 9 8 7 6 5 4 3 2 1

Keywords: Architecture, Barcelona, Beijing, bicycling, bus rapid transit, Curitiba, Paris, pedestrian zones, public markets, public space, public transportation, urbanism, urban planning

CONTENTS

PREFACE

It is with great pride that we present this English translation of Jaime Lerner's *Urban Acupuncture*. We know it belongs to the canon of great urban readings, and Jaime follows in the tradition of Jane Jacobs, William Whyte, and many other visionaries who have illuminated the world's thinking on cities. *Urban Acupuncture* is a work of fierce love for real, living, people-filled cities and cities for people.

Jaime's words emerge from knowing many cities and loving each of them for the surprises, delights, and kindness they offer, from the delight of a shaded sidewalk to the gift of a trumpeter who serenades his neighborhood every evening.

Jaime sees all these small wonders of a city and celebrates them. But Jaime is not just an observer. His love for cities bears fruit in a fierce devotion to making them work. He's an actor and a reinventor. He doesn't just preach urban acupuncture. As a mayor, an urban planner, and designer, he's actually successfully performed these interventions.

I share his love of cities and the wonder and possibilities that small interventions bring and how those pinpoints of action can reorder the fabric and sense of a city.

In Chicago, one of the cities I was fortunate to have called home, I had the pleasure of living three blocks from Lurie Garden. I considered myself the luckiest person in the world to be so near this urban oasis that was at once formal and wild, contemplative and quite alive. It was overwhelmingly beautiful, even in winter. Whenever I visited, and I tried to do so most days, I could feel my blood pressure drop. It was a respite of calm in a frenetic city.

(I've told my husband to please sneak my ashes in when I die and spread them there because it's a place where I could be quite content forever.)

Lurie was my calming point. Then there was Chicago's SummerDance. Set in a beautiful garden, it attracts the single most diverse group of people you could ever hope to gather. Strangers dance with strangers. And they touch each other for extended periods of time!

Evenings always begin with an hour of dance instruction, followed by two hours of dancing to live music. From June through September, Thursdays through Sundays, Chicagoans from all over town gather to dance Tango, Swing, Cajun, Rhumba, Salsa, Greek, Waltz, Step, Line, you name it. It's Chicago's own version of *Dancing with the*

Stars without the stars . . . just ordinary people who want to dance.

These two places, these two pinpoint interventions in time, space, and place have, for me, lifted the spirit and fabric of the city to sublime. Yes, real cities with real people will have real problems, but they will also have people like Jaime Lerner who are too busy loving their city and reinventing their community to let anything get in the way. As Jane Jacobs once put it, "Designing a dream city is easy. Rebuilding a living one takes imagination."

Knight Foundation wants to nurture civic innovators and we hope Jaime's words inspire more people to fully engage in the life of their city.

Carol Coletta
VP/Community and National Initiatives
The John S. and James L. Knight Foundation

FOREWORD

Without an understanding of people and politics, planning is merely a technocratic tool. Jaime Lerner has a deep understanding and passion for planning and politics—but he cares about people above all. In this book, he shares inspiring stories about how visions of unified and vibrant cities can become a reality through what he calls *urban acupuncture*.

We all know we have to work hard to create more sustainable and healthier cities. But it is one thing to agree upon those visions, and certainly another thing to do something meaningful about it. Transforming cities has to do with not only their physical features but also psychological, cultural, and many other factors. Jaime Lerner has been a great source of inspiration for generations of city planners and politicians as someone with a professional and human understanding of cities, but at the same time, a deep understanding of the political forces at work. It is therefore very much welcomed that he now shares his stories with a larger audience. With its poetic format, *Urban Acupuncture* is almost like getting a glimpse into Jaime Lerner's notebook, with stories from all over the world and from different periods in his career, including his work as a mayor as well as a consultant for cities around the globe.

Jaime Lerner is not only a good storyteller, he is a doer who has delivered impressive results and affected many people's lives in Curitiba and other cities. Urban acupuncture is an approach to city planning designed to make things happen. Don't start with everything, start somewhere, make things happen, try it out. The inspiration of this book and from Lerner is both visionary and very hands-on. Reading *Urban Acupuncture,* you get the feeling that you can actually make a difference; you can do it not alone, but together with others. Ways to bring all groups of citizens together are very much present in the book, and for good reasons, as the social, democratic aspects of urban life are of the utmost importance to make our cities work in the future as balanced communities for all.

This is not a technical or theoretical book; it is a book filled with poetry and magic that communicates the importance of dreaming and, at the same time, being pragmatic and making things happen; to always ask if we have the right solution or if there is a better, maybe a simpler way. Jaime Lerner is a much-needed advocate for simple, common-sense solutions—for example, Curitiba's system for guiding bus drivers to the correct position at bus stops. This solution could have become very complex and expensive, but ended up otherwise after a chat with a bus driver and a test showing that the driver could easily align his vehicle using lines painted on the bus window and platform.

The approach that people should be at the center of planning has been around for quite a number of years, and Jaime Lerner certainly is one of the pioneers within this field. It hasn't always been like that, however, and when Jaime Lerner proposed a pedestrian street in 1972 in Curitiba, it was not seen as the obvious thing. He describes how many business owners and other community members probably saw him as crazy. But only a day after the inauguration, one of the opponents requested that the work be extended and that the people-oriented approach be applied to other regions.

Lerner has always dared to take leadership; in this book, he shares stories that can inspire others to do the same. With the urban acupuncture approach, there are no excuses, and the focus is very much on getting started.

Good acupuncture is about understanding places better, understanding that one city is not like the other, understanding what it is that is missing in a neighborhood before designing. Here Lerner touches upon an important issue: the need for good programming. There is plenty of good design but an exorbitant lack of good programming with a deeper understating of problems, people, and places.

This book is like having a dinner with a good friend where the conversation just flows, one story after the other, good examples that will stick with you when you go home. One of those evenings when you go home inspired to do something yourself, believing that change can happen.

Thank you very much, Jaime Lerner.

Jan Gehl
Copenhagen, Denmark
May 2014

INTRODUCTION

I have always nurtured the dream and the hope that with the prick of a needle, diseases may be cured. The notion of restoring the vital signs of an ailing spot with a simple healing touch has everything to do with revitalizing not only that specific place but also the entire area that surrounds it.

I believe that some of the magic of medicine can and should be applied to cities, for many of them are ailing, and some are almost terminal. Just as good medicine depends on the interaction between doctor and patient, successful urban planning involves triggering healthy responses within the city, probing here and there to stimulate improvements and positive chain reactions. Intervention is all about revitalization, an indispensable way of making an organism function and change.

Street artist at the Centre Pompidou, Paris. Photo by K.C. Tang.
Creative Commons BY-SA 3.0.

I often ask myself how it is that some cities manage to make important and positive changes. There are scores of answers, but one seems to me to be common to all innovative cities: every city that succeeds has undergone an awakening, a new beginning. This is what makes a city respond.

Everyone knows that planning is a process. Yet no matter how good it may be, a plan by itself cannot bring about immediate transformation. Almost always, it is a spark that sets off a current that begins to spread. This is what I call *good acupuncture*—true *urban acupuncture.*

Where can we see examples of good urban acupuncture? San Francisco's revitalized Cannery district is one; another is Güell Park, in Barcelona. Sometimes, a pinpoint urban project leads to broader cultural changes, such as with the Centre Pompidou in Paris, or Frank Gehry's Guggenheim Bilbao museum, or even the restoration of Grand Central Station in New York.

Then again, urban acupuncture may also come in a single stroke of genius, such as the pyramids at the Louvre, the revitalization of Buenos Aires's Puerto Madero, or Oscar Niemeyer's Pampulha in Belo Horizonte. You can feel it at work in the smallest venues, like Paley Park in New York, or in grand structures like Jean Nouvel's Institute of the Arab World in Paris or Daniel Libeskind's Holocaust Museum in Berlin.

In some cases, interventions are made more out of dire necessity than out of a desire for improvement, and are meant to heal wounds that man has inflicted upon nature—the open wound of a rock quarry, for instance. In time, these urban scars may be transformed into a new landscape. Making the best of these new landscapes and repairing man's blunders requires nothing less than the best sort of acupuncture. One striking example is the Ópera de Arame, in Curitiba. Another is the removal of San Francisco's freeway.

Urban transit systems have administered admirable doses of urban acupuncture the world over. Consider the splendid gates of the centennial metro stations in Paris, Norman Foster's metro stations in Bilbao, or Curitiba's Express-Bus tube stations.

We know that the planning process of a city takes time—and it has to—for it involves a multitude of actors and issues, as well as long-term guidelines. However, sometimes, a simple, focused intervention can create new energy, demonstrating the possibilities of a space in a way that motivates others to engage with their community. It can even contribute to the planning process. This gets to the essence of true urban acupuncture—it needs to be precise and quick, that's the secret.

S.K. Deli, New York City. Photo by Dan DeLuca.

24-HOUR SHOPKEEPERS IN NEW YORK CITY

Urban acupuncture doesn't always have to involve bricks and mortar. Sometimes it follows the introduction of a new custom or a change of habit that suddenly clears the way to transformation. Often good urban acupuncture arises from unplanned human intervention, where no bulldozer or construction crew has ever trodden.

I often say that New York should build a monument to the Unknown 24-hour Shopkeeper. This industrious group—many of them immigrants from Korea—has done the city an extraordinary service merely by keeping its grocery stores and sidewalk delicatessens open around the clock. These shops not only offer infinite shelves of merchandise but also enliven whole neighborhoods by literally lighting up countless dreary street corners. People mingle and meet under the glow of city lights as they go out for nighttime shopping. And all of this makes for a much safer city.

And since these shopkeepers never sleep, their blazing storefronts serve as vital city reference points doing far more for the city than any parade or cultural festival ever could. This is why the unknown shopkeeper and the myriad mom-and-pop businesses rank among the finest acupuncturists of New York.

Many of the stores in New York's "Little Korea" recall the charms of Les Halles in the wee hours of predawn Paris. For decades, this market was the heart of the city, a pulse beating away for generation after generation, much like the night markets that keep the streets glowing after dark in thousands of cities around the world. To this day, a small open-air market survives on Paris's Rue de Seine at the corner of Bucci, a hallowed urban address that time has not erased.

In the East, there are many more examples, starting with the Tokyo fish market, which is aboil with commerce long before the sun comes up. Here giant octopuses are on display; there stingrays spread their great wings over ice. Everywhere buyers and sellers haggle and hawk their wares, a Babel of commerce that announces each new day.

I often say that all these people who toil away at daybreak are urban orderlies, pumping oxygen into cities that must never be allowed to stop breathing. They are a city's true lifeblood.

Cine Teatro Morretes in Morretes, Brazil. Photo by Anna Carolina Russo.

THE OLD CINEMA NOVO

One feature common to all good urban acupuncture is the imperative of preserving or restoring the cultural identity of a place or a community. So many cities today need acupuncture because they have neglected their cultural identity. A sad example is the disappearance of the local movie theater.

In the past, the movie house was the magic realm of fantasy, music, utopia, reality, dreams, and hope. Above all, cinemas were places for city residents to meet and mingle.

Movie theatres influenced entire generations, and not just culturally; they were places where people gathered, gossiped, laughed, and argued, their discussions often echoing late into the night and reverberating in other parts of town. Cinemas helped spread fashion and fads, literature and dance, music and even history. And nothing rivals the movie house when it comes to recording the important dates of a nation.

Movie theaters had their own stories to tell and became part of urban history. Yet in most cities around the world they are disappearing. In scores of towns, the old movie house has given way to supermarkets, churches, and so on. Too often, the traditional movie house has been replaced by shopping mall cineplexes; but that is another story.

A city's memory is like an old family portrait. And just as we wouldn't think of tearing up an old family picture—and the old movie theatre is part of this picture—we can't afford to lose this point of reference, which is so vital to our own identity.

In the state of Paraná in southern Brazil, a project has been launched to restore old movie theatres. These restored theatres are equipped with the latest in movie projection and viewing technology, thereby creating new venues for national film festivals and independent productions that are so often neglected by the major studios and the shopping mall cineplex.

In this way, the old Cinema Novo is a program that reinforces our cultural identity. This is urban acupuncture trying to recuperate our collective loss of memory and identity.

Umbrellas hang above the revitalized Cheonggyecheon River in Seoul, South Korea. Photo by Diana Lim, www.flickr.com/traveloriented.

RESCUING A RIVER

When I first arrived in Seoul some years ago, the South Korean capital appeared to hold few surprises. Here was one more ancient Asian city transformed by an impressive vitality, hurtling vertiginously into modernity; so much so that you might never have guessed this city dated back 800 years.

Pedestrians admire an art installation in the Cheonggyecheon River.
Photo by riNux, Flickr. Creative Commons BY-SA 2.0.

Seoul was another example of a place where things were done in a hurry: huge avenues and freeways speeding toward a chaotic downtown where people have to dive in and out of underground passages just to cross the street. The cars, meanwhile, rolled over unblemished pavement, almost as if gliding on a red carpet.

This is how so many cities were built, and destroyed, by kowtowing to the combustion engine. Beautiful, historic cities, each one appointed with magnificent buildings and palaces, and surrounded by our modern-day dragons—automobiles.

My first surprise in Seoul was being invited to observe a rare urban initiative. The mayor's office wanted to set aside a major portion of the city's streets for the Curitiba Bus, a mass transportation system anchored by an express bus and known as the BRT, or Bus Rapid Transit.

The greatest surprise of all: the Seoul government planned to remove the spaghetti-like tangle of elevated highways from the transit-choked downtown area and revive a stream, the Cheonggyecheon, which once captured the runoff from the winter thaw from the surrounding slopes. The stream—believe it or not—had been bulldozed decades before in order to hide the degradation and pollution that had beset it over the years. The elevated ways were built on top of reclaimed areas.

Now the plan was to restore the site by salvaging the river and revitalizing the adjacent areas. The project was expensive (repairing a mess is never cheap), but the enthusiasm of the mayor and his staff was compelling. Their plan also included making way for pedestrians (a people-friendly city).

As soon as we arrived, we were shown the projects. All of the planners, architects, and engineers involved demonstrated a very sharp understanding of the city: its design was clear, incorporating the hillsides and the revitalized stream. That is to say, the renewed city was already in their heads. I had no doubt that soon enough their projects would come to life as well, as they in fact did. The road infrastructure was removed to reveal the river and its course, creating an area where people and the natural environment could interact again, and reestablishing an important reference for the city.

In Seoul, I also had the privilege of sitting down with one of the city's most respected intellects—Young-Oak Kim—a philosopher with a Harvard degree who went on to study medicine. After returning to his native land, Professor Kim taught philosophy for two years in one of the most popular courses in South Korea. Now this very famous man has decided to be a reporter, looking into major issues. Our conversation was a celebration. We shared so many ways of thinking, and especially a belief in simplicity—the essence of Eastern philosophy.

During our visit, Professor Kim drew for me a free-hand map of the city. What impressed me most was how closely he "read" the city, citing the meaning of each neighborhood, of each location, and of every name, all done so simply and concisely. Like the engineers of the Cheonggyecheon restoration, Professor Kim understands the elements of the city like few others can. If only all cities had fewer peddlers of complexity and more philosophers!

Cyclists on a Beijing street, fall 1988. Photo by John R. Williams. Accessed via IDEAS: Image Database to Enhance Asian Studies.

THE FORBIDDEN CITY

History tells us that Beijing is one of the world's oldest cities. In the early fifteenth century, it was divided into two cities, separated by walls. The inner city cradled the Imperial City, surrounded by a 10-km wall. This was

"The Forbidden City," where moats marked the perimeters of the palaces of emperors. The last emperor was Pu-Yi, overthrown in 1911 and expelled from the city in 1924.

But Beijing has lost one of its most striking features. The sea of bicycles that was part of the traditional landscape has disappeared. On each bicycle sat one person, or maybe more. It was a city of people.

Today's Beijing is more like an encampment of ultra modern buildings, surrounded by enormous freeways, by-passes, clover leaves, and beltways. In the "donut" formed by the second and third beltway rings, there's a Central Business District. Beijing is now a city of roads.

Close to the Forbidden City and in some immediately adjacent areas, it's still possible to make out small sections of what used to be the old city—a city that today is preserved only in old movies and books.

Beijing needs a good dose of urban acupuncture to reclaim its rightful place in the sun. That means fewer highways, less concrete, and more room for people and bicycles. Just a pinprick here and there might be enough to bring back the old-fashioned streets and the city buses. How presumptuous of me! Trying to teach acupuncture to the Chinese!

Children in Santiago de Cali, Colombia. Photo by Romano Germán Barney.

CALI

Like clockwork, a breeze wafts in announcing the evening. A plaza glows softly under the stars. The city is safe and peaceful as lovers stroll and children skip along the sidewalks. Here and there, you can still glimpse the city's soul: the old neighborhoods, the soft colors, the sidewalks echoing the beat of a distant *salsa*.

Parque de la Retreta at night, Santiago de Cali. Photo by Romano Germán Barney.

What a shame a good part of this Colombian city's identity has been lost amid so many outsized avenues. Just to cross them, you'll find yourself huffing up and over suspended pedestrian bridges.

Suddenly, you stumble across an old open-air shopping mall with internal gardens, a large courtyard with live acoustic music, and not an amplifier in sight. There's no piped-in soundtrack beating down on your head.

It's devilishly hot, but by four-thirty or five in the afternoon, a soft breeze comes whispering over the city. Perhaps it's the gods themselves who are calling at last.

But there's good architecture in Cali. There it was in a small house I visited, built by architect Benjamín Barney and measuring barely 6 meters wide, with a patio. Or rather, I should say the house *is* the patio, embraced by several balconies.

Maybe, in this city good acupuncture means building things smaller and stepping aside to give way to the simple beauties of nature, like the handsome river or the caressing wind.

Chévere!

The Santa Justa Elevator, Lisboa, Portugal. Photo by Nol Aders. Creative Commons BY-SA 3.0.

DO NOTHING! URGENTLY

One of the first decisions I had to make in my first term as mayor of Curitiba was how to respond to a petition presented by a neighborhood association, which made a rather odd request. They asked that the city do nothing in that particular neighborhood.

I sent the secretary of public works to check into the situation. What we discovered was that the association's request, though highly unusual, made good sense. The city was tidying up the area—aligning the still unpaved streets—but what concerned the residents was that the machines might end up covering a small natural spring.

My directive to the public works authority was terse but unequivocal: "Do nothing! Urgently." Sometimes, when a city faces decisions about public works that could do more harm than good, doing nothing is the most urgent priority.

Thirty-two years later, while driving around Lisbon, I looked at the hills, Lisbon's beautiful hills, and at the river Tejo. The day's newspaper carried a story about new projects for Lisbon—tunnels and overpasses. Expo 98 had blessed the city with improvements, but mostly by aggressively renovating a blighted part of the city.

In the classical Lisbon—Avenidas Liberdade, Rocio and Colinas—maybe the best acupuncture calls for doing nothing at all, urgently.

P.S. Almost nothing, that is. How about a brazen bit of meddling? Say, painting the Santa Justa Elevator in vermilion?

Avenida da Liberdade at night. Photo by Emilio García.

Rua 24 horas, Curitiba. Photo by Morio. Creative Commons BY-SA 3.0

AROUND THE CLOCK,
OR THE 24-HOUR CITY

It's late afternoon in Zócalo, Mexico City's old historic district, and suddenly, I get the feeling I'm going to be swallowed up in the crowd. People sluice back and forth like floodwaters. Most of them are street vendors peddling odds

Street seafood in Bangkok's Chinatown. Photo by John Walker.

and ends, just trying to stay afloat themselves. Suddenly, a question hits me broadside in this human riptide: how in the world can a megacity reconcile the formal and informal sectors of the economy? So far, the answers we've come up with have been mostly fruitless if not outright unjust.

So why not call a truce to allow the two rival economies to work together? Since the day has 24 hours, the first step might be to strike an agreement to decide who works when.

Street vendors could start after hours—at say 6:00 pm, their colorful mobile stalls livening up the city as the signs go dark on many conventional storefronts. This could be a rare win-win combination for cities. One sector would help the other because both would work in sequence, keeping the city alive with commerce day and night. The round-the-clock buzz of commerce would not only please consumers but might even make the streets safer.

Street peddlers, after all, represent an institution as old as the city itself. Think of open-air markets. At a given hour, in a given neighborhood, street merchants go to work—often hours before the lights go on in traditional storefronts—and then vanish along with their wares and jerry-built booths, leaving hardly a trace.

And this arrangement works out fairly well. The open market is a moveable feast that rises early and packs up with the sun. Some cities, like Shanghai, Hong Kong, and Curitiba, have nighttime street markets. These make for pleasant rendezvous points during the less hectic hours.

Here acupuncture is performed according to the ticking of the clock.

Christmas lights of Rua XV de Novembro, Curitiba. Photo by Radamés Manosso.

URBAN KINDNESS

Some years ago, a group of exceptional people from Belo Horizonte, my old friend Valério Fabris among them, managed to win respect by promoting initiatives that encouraged people to demonstrate love for their city. Call them the promoters of urban kindness.

Since then, there's been a steady flow of creative ideas and gestures reflecting the growing community awareness that urban kindness is essential to the livelihood of any city.

One storied example is the Little Cow of Leopoldina Street—a sculpture in a city park that was "adopted" by Belo Horizonte's residents. Some time ago, vandals attacked the cow and almost destroyed it. But one man took it upon himself to cross the city with a bucket of sand and cement and rebuild it. Now and again, the Little Cow sports a new look and new colors whenever the artistic impulse seizes the townspeople who have grown so fond of her.

One housewife in the São Geraldo district is famous for the nativity scene she sets up in her living room every Christmas. She never locks her door and gladly welcomes anyone who wants to visit her yuletide installation. In another Belo Horizonte neighborhood, garbage collectors sing while they work. This is how urban kindness became a tradition in the capital of Minas Gerais.

There are people who go about their business with pleasure or make no secret of the joy they take in their everyday lives.

By placing his sculptures on the sand of Leme beach in Rio de Janeiro, Oscar Niemeyer also made a gracious bow to urban kindness.

In Curitiba, after finishing his daily work, one dentist goes to his office window and plays the trumpet.

In Porto Alegre, a radio station has a window looking on the Rua da Praia, where passersby can gather and watch live interviews. Inviting the public to look over your shoulder while you work is a true example of urban kindness.

When I worked in Rio de Janeiro, there was a talented designer on our team. I will never forget the day he came to the office dressed as a clown. He took his seat at his desk and quietly worked away all day long, just as he always did. Late that afternoon, he announced that he was quitting his job because he had decided to do what he had always dreamed of doing: become a circus clown. Without telling a soul, it seemed, he had been studying after hours to be a clown. That's when he drew his first round of applause.

Some years ago, I went out to hear the superb Hélcio Milito bossa nova trio. That was a long time ago, but I will always remember that evening's gesture of urban kindness. After the show, the club's owner, seeing that I was having difficulties hailing a cab at that late hour, drove me to my hotel in his own car.

Then there is Maripá, a small city in the west of my home state of Paraná, where town officials had orchids planted along the streets. These flowers were so pretty that towns-people returned the favor by implanting their own code of urban courtesy: nobody messes with Maripá's orchids.

In Rome, my dear friend Domenico de Masi once told me another fine story of urban kindness. Every Friday, a group of residents in a certain apartment building organizes the exhibit of a painter in the elevator; you can admire the painting as you ride. But the experience isn't confined to the elevator shaft. As you go back down the stairs, you ring the bell of all the apartments on each floor. One by one, the residents open their doors and talk about the painting and tell stories about the artist over coffee. Once a week, the painting is replaced by a new one by a different artist. It just goes to show that urban kindness can also be beautiful.

In Salvador, Carlinhos Brown founded a music school in a shantytown, where every Saturday he sponsors a live concert by local musicians. A recording company records a CD of the show and the profits go to the inhabitants.

My son-in-law, Bas, once told me a story about the "window-washers' floating gardens," in New York. One architect came up with the idea of placing plants and flower boxes on the elevated platforms that window washers use to clean outside windows. As the platforms hover alongside the building, they turn into true floating gardens. This is an unforgettable kindness.

Back in the 1980s, the city of Curitiba decorated its buses for the Christmas season. The moving strings of lights and illuminated Christmas trees were a colorful gift for those who had to spend Christmas day working. And as the buses made their rounds, they ended up spreading the light of Christmas to the entire city.

Sometimes urban kindness is embodied by a single person, like the late Sérgio Mercer. His fellow townspeople regarded Mercer as a man of sterling character, a talented advertising executive, and an extremely skilled writer. His death was a very sad moment in the life of Curitiba.

Mercer was a special kind of Curitibano. He somehow embodied the face and the consciousness of the city. He knew everything there is to know about music, literature, and was also a great cultural critic. Above all else, he was a loyal friend. And Mercer had another extraordinary talent, as well: he was a conversation tuner. If the conversation in a group started to go flat, Mercer would fine-tune it to a more agreeable key.

He had the habit of orchestrating, and could come up with new arrangements anywhere, anytime. He loved the tango and played an imaginary *bandonéon*. You could actually see him "playing" it; the velvet band on the knee and all.

The whole city turned out for his funeral to reminisce about one of its dearest characters. One of his cousins spotted me there and gave me a rare CD of tangos: "I was saving it for Mercer, but since he is no longer here, I would like you, one of his best friends, to have it."

Then I remembered that I also had bought a tango anthology that I meant to give to Mercer. I left the cemetery with a heavy heart.

On the way home I stopped at a restaurant for takeout, since none of my family was in the mood for going out that day. Then I bumped into Monica Rischbieter and her friends, all of whom were glum after the funeral. Then it occurred to me to give Monica the book that I had been saving for Mercer.

That led me to the idea of launching a Mercer's National Day, a date set aside for giving a friend a gift. The date would be May 6, the day when all of Curitiba lost a great friend. Since we could no longer give Mercer gifts, we would honor him by giving presents to one another.

It would have been the greatest sort of urban kindness, and a fitting tribute to the man who always gave so much to his city.

Vampeta, a soccer star who used to play for the Brazilian national team, also offered a fine gesture of urban kindness to his home town, tiny Nazaré das Farinhas, tucked away in the northeastern state of Bahia. Once, when he was passing through his hometown, someone asked him if he could spare 20 reais (about $11) to help patch up the movie theatre's leaky roof.

Vampeta decided to have a look and quickly saw that the building that housed the cinema was in deplorable shape. In fact, the Cine Rio Branco was a town landmark, one of Brazil's oldest surviving movie houses, dating to 1927. So Vampeta bought the building and totally refurbished it. They say that the inauguration of the new cinema was the biggest celebration Narzaré had ever had, with soccer legend Ronaldinho on hand as honored guest.

The movie house still does not turn much of a profit. So Vampeta pays the salaries of its employees out of his own pocket. In addition to showing films, the theater also stages plays and holds art workshops for more than eighty children who live in nearby slums. Vampeta himself doesn't even like the movies, but he never thought twice about offering this gesture of urban kindness to his hometown.

Tango dancers in the San Telmo neighborhood of Buenos Aires, Argentina. Photo by Luiz Cavalheiros.

MUSICAL ACUPUNCTURE

In Antonina, a coastal city in the state of Paraná, they serve a delicious dish that is cooked in a clay pot sealed with manioc purée. They call it the *barreado*. By local tradition, fireworks announce the opening of the pot. But what makes the occasion even more special is that the city's anthem is sung as the pot is unsealed.

Every city has its own gesture, its own song. Some have a whole repertoire that immediately brings to mind the town's

Street musicians in Rome. Photo by Marco Heersink, Studio 2255.

particular features and landscape. Think of Rio and you are likely to start humming "Copacabana," "Corcovado," "Girl From Ipanema," or "Cidade Maravilhosa."

Rome, Chicago, New York, San Francisco—all these cities have been immortalized by songs that, in time, became universal. When you hear them, you instantly evoke a mental portrait of the city.

Just mention tango, or Carlos Gardel, and Buenos Aires automatically comes to mind. You can take in a tango show almost anywhere these days, for there are accomplished *tangeros* the world over, but nothing compares to a show in Buenos Aires, where the genre was born. No matter where it turns up, tango will always carry its *porteño* stamp of origin.

Samba is one of Rio de Janeiro's cultural trademarks. There are professional samba musicians all over the country. But come Carnival, samba takes its rightful place, in the streets. And that is where Rio—with its choreographed parades of 80,000 or more costumed dancers, dancing and singing in the world's largest opera—is unbeatable.

When a distinct song or beat takes hold of a city's or country's identity, then good urban acupuncture is at work. It has echoes in everyday living, like the improvised tapping on a matchbox at a street bar in Rio, the beat of drums on the sidewalks of Bahia, or hip-hop gushing from the giant boom boxes in the streets of New York.

Some songs are in themselves a form of acupuncture. Others have become veritable tattoos—by ⌐   Gil, Caetano Veloso, Milton Nascimento. ⌐   and Vinicius de Moraes—adding ⸱   city's features.

It is hard to imagine   at Caymmi, João Gilberto, Gil, and Caetano. /   uld Minas be without the music of Milton Nas

Brazil wouldn't be   nout Villa-Lobos or Ary Barroso.

There are songs that pra tically seem to conjure the city before you, as though they were mental snapshots.

But leave it to Antonio Carlos Jobim to write music that made his storied city, Rio de Janeiro, seem even more beautiful. And by looking better, a city becomes better.

Craft market in Bryant Park, New York City. Photo by Stacy Cashman at RamblingTraveler.com. Creative Commons BY-SA 2.0.

CONTINUITY IS LIFE

Many major urban problems arise from a lack of continuity. A city pocked with lifeless suburbs or tracts of urban real estate devoid of housing is just as skewed as one strewn with abandoned lots and ramshackle buildings. Filling up these many urban "voids" can be the first step to sound acupuncture.

An important step is to add elements that may be missing from a given area. If there is plenty of commerce or industry but no people, then housing development could be encouraged. If another district is all homes and apartment blocks, why not boost services? And if a building is crumbling or a shop closes its doors, something new must be built in its place, even if it's only temporary. Some years ago, after watching some of Curitiba's traditional coffee houses— true meeting points in the city—go out of business, we built a provisional café in a pedestrian mall that served as new hub of activity.

The quicker an abandoned lot is occupied, the better, and preferably with something even more attractive or lively than before. I am also in favor of creating temporary structures to rescue failing services or establishments—say a flower market or a concert hall—until new projects take hold. You could call this jerry-built acupuncture: putting up portable structures here and there to shore up threatened neighborhoods or city addresses that need revitalizing or a new burst of energy.

The key is to add the urban function that is missing. It could be building homes or else creating a provisional recreation center; the goal is to promote a healthy mix of urban activities. Whatever structures are constructed, any initiative must be undertaken quickly so as not to break the continuity of urban life. Continuity *is* life.

Lobster vendor in Sihanoukville, Cambodia. Photo by Tartarin2009, Flickr. Creative Commons BY 2.0.

STREET SOUNDS, COLORS, AND SCENTS

Street vendors are, for the most part, an unloved class. That's a shame, because they are more than just another kind of mobile merchant. Granted, sometimes their practices fall shy of the norms of conventional commerce. But given how prevalent these footloose vendors are in our lives, perhaps it's time they were regarded with a little more sympathy.

Whether it's New York's roving hot-dog chefs, barefoot merchants peddling coconut milk or sunscreen on the beaches of Rio, or the fruit sellers in the Caribbean who balance towering baskets of produce on their heads, street sellers everywhere share a common identity. They infuse sound, aroma, and color into the city streets in a way that defines and enlivens our everyday lives.

For years, I lived in front of a cookie factory in Cabral, a district in my hometown of Curitiba. Every day of the week, a different type of cookie was baked. Thursday was coconut-cookie day, and the savory perfume of toasted coconut permeated the entire neighborhood.

The factory is no longer there, but every Thursday I can still smell those coconut cookies baking. Likewise, on Curitiba's south side, the air is laced with the pungent smell of *matte* tea from the tea factory there. People around the world have similar stories to tell about their own cities.

The hum of roaming knife sharpeners honing blades, the chant of fruit vendors, paperboys crying out the latest headlines: by now some of these sounds may have completely disappeared from cities.

But new signs appear. The "sandwich-board" men of São Paulo and so many other cities, who hawked their wares on facing billboards worn around their necks like twin slices of bread, have given way to fancy websites on which countless opportunities are now advertised.

But the sounds, the colors, the aromas of open-air markets and of street vendors must not be allowed to disappear.

What a terrible place is a flavorless city, leeched of the spice and color that are the essence of its soul.

Teatro Paiol, Curitiba. Photo by Janaina Falkiewicz/janafalk, Flickr.

GOOD RECYCLING

Each city has its history, its own points of reference. I am not just referring to all those landmark buildings that are part of any nation's heritage. I mean the places that belong to the city's collective memory and that are vital to its identity—the intangible bond that forges a sense of belonging. It might be a particular factory, an old tram station, or one of those bygone general stores with its wares scattered unpretentiously over creaky shelves.

But since many of these once-familiar urban icons are gone forever or changed beyond recognition, we have to come up with new ones and new activities to bring our dormant city spaces back to life. There is nothing that flatters a neighborhood—indeed, an entire community—more than the revival of such "lost" spaces.

San Francisco led the way in the late 1960s when it transformed the old Ghirardelli chocolate factory and the long-shuttered Del Monte cannery into Ghirardelli Square and The Cannery, which blossomed into vibrant public arcades. Both are now key attractions of San Francisco's storied Fisherman's Wharf.

Beginning in the 1970s, urban recycling began to sweep the globe, with brilliant projects like São Paulo's SESC theatre complex, London's train stations, and so many other restored treasures across Europe.

In 1971, Curitiba converted its old powder house into a small theater, the Teatro Paiol. Soon after, an old glue factory was reincarnated as the Creativity Center, a civic recreational arts center.

And who could deny the charms of Puerto Madero, the old Buenos Aires docks transformed into a stylish riverside arcade and office complex or São Paulo's Julio Prestes Station, which was reinvented as a splendid concert hall.

There are good and bad examples of urban recycling, of course. What matters is that the worldwide wave of revitalization has rescued our cities by turning blighted urban zones into vital new civic spaces. This is great acupuncture.

Now even grave injuries inflicted by man on the urban landscape—abandoned quarries and craters created by sandblasting—have been refashioned into handsome parks and amphitheaters. Once again, Curitiba led the way with its Ópera de Arame (an opera house made of glass and lightweight steel), and the Pedreira Paulo Leminski (an open-air amphitheater built to accommodate 80,000 spectators), and scores of other parks built in honor of the myriad ethnic groups and immigrants who forged the city's cultural life.

Even the Iguaçu River valley, with its ring of surrounding ponds, helped salvage the whole state from a terrible ecological disaster. Once an oil spill in the Iguaçu River threatened to blight the landscape, but the necklace of small connecting lakes saved the day, serving as a natural filter. The oil slick overran the first pond and then another and another; but finally the tenth sandy-bottomed pond did the job, halting the damage and allowing rescue workers to begin an intensive clean up. Divine intervention? Hardly. These ponds were nothing but the wounds man had inflicted upon the landscape while quarrying for sand.

Here, injury became a solution. Thanks to these unintended ponds, man designed a new life for the Iguaçu River.

Shibuya Crossing, Tokyo, Japan. Photo by Candida.Performa, Flickr.
Creative Commons BY 2.0.

PEOPLE IN THE STREETS

Sometimes, I stop to watch how a drop of molasses draws a swarm of ants. Or how a bar or a general store in a poor neighborhood—with their blazing lights and animation—attracts people. In fact, it's mainly people who attract people. Man is both a protagonist and a spectator in the drama of everyday life unfolding on the city stage.

Good acupuncture is about drawing people out to the streets and creating meeting places. Mainly, it is about helping the city become a catalyst of interactions between people. A mass transit hub, for example, doesn't have to be just a bus station. It can also be a gathering place.

In Strasbourg, the inviting design of the tram stops makes for pleasant points of rendezvous and leisure. In Seoul, I saw a metro station that houses an infant recreation area and a small planetarium. In Curitiba, buzzing bus terminals, where between 500,000 and 800,000 passengers come and go each day, have become agreeable public malls.

The more cities are understood to be the integration of functions—bringing together rich and poor, the elderly and the young—the more meeting places they will create and the livelier they will become. The design of public space is important. Place de la Bourse in Lyon; Barcelona's Plaza del Sol; the Gammeltorv in Copenhagen; Tokyo's Tsukuba Centre Square; and the Pioneer Courthouse Square in Portland, Oregon, are magnificent examples of how to transform the city by creating dynamic and inviting public spaces.

Getting students into the streets is also hugely important. In too many cities around the world, students are physically severed from the heartbeat of urban life, confined to distant islands that are conventionally known as campuses.

Sometimes, the space is so barren that it is more like a desert. It's just the opposite of what students really need: to be integrated with the city in order to develop a more generous view of society. Otherwise, all they'll get are fragments of information about a world they know only from a distance instead of through daily experience. After all, can you imagine the Sorbonne far from Paris, or Columbia University in some New York exurb, or Berkeley severed from San Francisco? What would the University of Heidelberg or São Paulo School of Law be if they were somehow uprooted and plunked down far away from their vibrant cities?

And if universities seem remote and self-contained, why not bring the campus to the town by sponsoring public seminars or arts and cultural events for the broader community? In the same way, the university campus can return the favor and open its gates to the city. One way or another, town and gown work best not as rivals but as partners.

Jaime Lerner with a Dock Dock car, an electric car-sharing service in Paris. Photo courtesy of Instituto Jaime Lerner.

SMART CAR, SMART BUS

Few topics are more hotly debated today than that of the future of transportation. Much of the talk centers on the car of the future, and judging by the ever-more-sophisticated automobile shows around the world, the vehicle of the future looks daring indeed. Even the Museum of Modern Art weighed in on the discussion some three years ago with a major exhibit dedicated to the technology and design of the car of tomorrow.

But the true *smart* car still hasn't been invented. When carmakers unveil a bold new design, the engine is fairly standard, while the models boasting advanced engines (the hybrid and flex-fuel varieties) aren't much to look at. Cars tailored to city driving—petite, fuel-efficient, and slow—are lousy on the open highway. Well, if two different types of cars are really required, then why not build two cars in one:

a car/bike, say, or even a sedan with another collapsible city car folded in the trunk?

After all, the Smart Bus already exists. It comes with a few basic features and requirements. First, it requires a lane all its own (painted or not, but exclusive nonetheless), a reliable schedule, and frequent runs. Next, there must be stepless boarding and exit ways, prepaid ticketing, and a choice of local or express lines arriving and departing at regular intervals.

I have no doubt that the city of the future will be served by surface transit. It is faster, vastly cheaper (one-hundredth the cost per kilometer of a subway), and can be easily integrated with existing metro lines. The secret is to create a bus service that performs as efficiently as or better than a subway line. The solution? The BRT.

The Smart Bike also exists. This is a bicycle that doesn't have to jostle for space among cars, trucks, or buses in the street, or crowd out pedestrians on the sidewalk. It is a bike with a path of its own, a clearly marked trail that follows rivers, canals, and railroad tracks. This bike will only become truly intelligent, however, when it's as easy to use as, well, an umbrella; just pop it out, press a lever and, *voilá*, instant portable transportation.

Then there's the Smart Taxi, a vehicle that competes neither with the bus nor the metro. It doesn't vie for the same space or customers as the other means of transportation, but complements both. In this way, the Smart Taxi helps keep traffic flowing by ferrying passengers to and fro from the subway to the nearest integrated bus station, or between subway hubs without trying to replace or upstage either service. In order to mesh well with the larger public transit web, the Smart Taxi would have to operate on the same integrated fare system. Imagine that—cabs working in partnership with mass transportation and not against it!

Now, imagine the ultimate mode of transportation: the Smart Pedestrian. Smart pedestrians are those who are allowed to move freely throughout the city, even in city parking lots, just by flashing their own personalized mobility card. As a consumer, the Smart Pedestrian will demand efficient urban facilities, more shops, and better services. Of course, they will have to be smart shops, smart movie theaters, and smart services.

Morros dos Prazeres favela, Rio de Janeiro. Photo by Dany13, Flickr. Creative Commons BY 2.0.

COMMITMENT TO SOLIDARITY

Is it possible to practice sound urban acupuncture and still be committed to social solidarity? For decades, we have lived with the consequences of social inequality, which ends up marginalizing a considerable segment of low-income people in cities. Just the paperwork churned out by countless seminars, symposia, and consultancies on the urban underclasses would be enough to cover up a large part of the world's slums.

Most of the world's poor make their homes on hillsides or in the lowlands. It was the best they could do in societies that left them little alternative. But what now? How to take urban infrastructure to these inhospitable areas? What is to be done with the garbage that piles up into polluting mountains that occasionally collapse, burying whole communities? Can we find a way to provide honest work for the jobless and the underemployed? Most important, how can we stop the twin modern urban epidemics of drugs and violence?

Some cities are showing the way. Curitiba, for example, solved its waste problem in deprived areas by encouraging residents to exchange their garbage for bus tokens. The system was founded over thirteen years ago and has been working ever since.

About twenty-five years ago, I came up with a plan for taking infrastructure to hillside *favelas*. The idea called for using the handrails of the paths and stairs that usually wind their way up through the slums as conduits for water pipes and electrical cables, branching off to feed individual homes through the rooftops or windows.

Sewer pipes, meantime, would be channeled along the base of the stairway. It was a simple and practical solution, but came with one major caveat: no digging into hillsides was allowed, because it could increase the risk of landslides.

And there's more. The level areas of hillside districts could be equipped with recreational and commercial facilities and community services, just like any other area of the city. Jobs could be created by turning the favelas into duty-free zones, with tax breaks for manufacturing and service industries operating in the slums. Such tax-free zones would attract investments and services from other neighborhoods, helping to integrate the favelas with the rest of the city. In this way, enterprise in the hills and the lowlands would radiate out to the entire city, creating opportunities and, undoubtedly, helping to reduce violence and crime.

The best way to bring safety to the slums is to generate business opportunities in the most densely populated districts and the flatlands. Restaurants, shops, service centers, streetlights, and other urban facilities are all beacons of integration. Forget all the elaborate diagnostics and endless urban study groups. Taking social integration up the hillsides is a good and expedient kind of urban acupuncture.

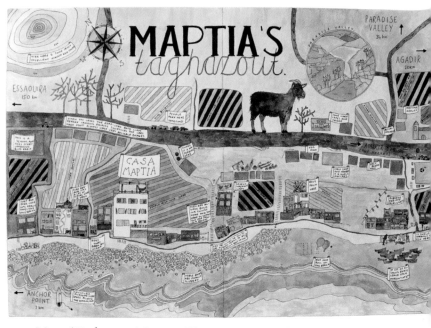

Map of Taghazout, Morocco. Illustration accessed via Maptia and drawn by Ella F. Sanders (ellafrancessanders.com).

DRAW YOUR CITY

G ood urban acupuncture is also the art of stimulating knowledge about the city. How many of us really know the city in which we live? And since we rarely pay much mind to what we don't know, how can we hope to generate respect for a city we don't understand?

Draw your city. That's what I suggested to 200 journalists gathered in Cali for International Journalist's Day. To what extent do reporters who write about and comment on the urban beat day in and day out have a broad view of the town they cover?

What I was trying to tell the journalists that day was that city reporting is not only about whether the mayor is a hero or a crook. Rather, I wanted to know how stories about the city's failings might be of value. What I hoped was for the journalists to tell me how they thought their work might really help the city.

But how can you improve your city if you don't even know it? Or don't draw it? That's what's most important: We get to know the city by a few of its streets and points of reference. City maps—which, in any case, so few of us know—are little more than lines on a grid. I began to learn about the rivers of my city only when I started working as an architect in the municipal urban planning department.

The same applies to state (or province) and country maps. What is depicted is a political blueprint of municipalities, a jigsaw puzzle whose pieces fit together to form a state, a country. But this state, this country has a design that has nothing to do with this puzzle. It is the design of its rivers, hills, plateaus, and mountain ridges where natural resources are located.

Of course, those who cannot see this tend to get their knowledge from others. But it is not the same thing. Draw your city. Make a model of your state. Draw your country.

Some time ago, when I was state governor, I launched a campaign with the purpose of encouraging everybody to help to preserve our rivers. Since the major polluting factors were sewers—the government's responsibility—and garbage, this was something the people could take charge of.

During this campaign children were asked: Do you know the river that flows near your house? How could they respect these rivers if they didn't even know them?

And what's worse, almost all of the rivers were covered, channeled.

Once the rivers were identified, the idea was to write down the name of the river running near their houses by the house number. Maybe then, people would start preserving them.

At the Science Park, built in Curitiba as a means of recovering the old facilities of a rural trade-show park, we installed, among other things, a huge model of the state of Paraná. A walk through the model gives you more knowledge than months of history and geography studies.

In that same park we built a planetarium showing how indigenous peoples saw the universe and its constellations. This wonderful idea cost only ten thousand dollars, a very low sum compared to the cost of a traditional planetarium.

If ancient stargazers could see these constellations drawn in the sky and hand down this knowledge from generation to generation, why shouldn't you be able to draw your own city? Making such a drawing would be good urban acupuncture. Once assimilated, it would become a beautiful imprint of a memory.

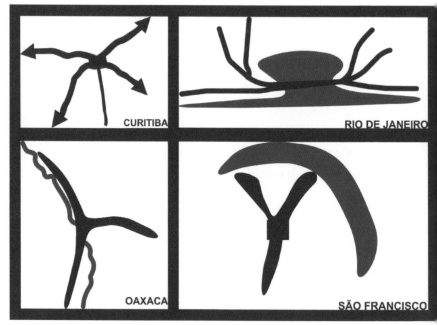

Illustration courtesy of Instituto Jaime Lerner.

INSTRUCTIONS FOR PERFORMING
URBAN ACUPUNCTURE

Don't forget that the city is a meeting point. It is gregarious by definition, the place where the codes and by-laws of living together were first established.

The great ideological conflict in the world today is "globalization vs. solidarity." In the words of Portugal's Mario Soares, we must "globalize solidarity."

And the city is the last refuge of solidarity. The city isn't the problem—it's the solution.

The biggest problem we created was moving our livelihoods away from our homes. We separated work from life.

The city is an integrated structure of life and work. The city is a melting pot of human activities. The more you blend incomes, ages, and activities, the more human the city becomes.

Imagine a city in layers deposited over time, and it's like searching for its hidden design; a strange archeology that revives ancient buildings, streets, and meeting spots, assigning new functions, changing values we once held dear. It's like gazing into a kaleidoscope and finding the lost design that will enable us to better understand present encounters.

We can give this design something new, consolidating it with mass transportation, adequate land use and a framework of roadways, all bound together in a single purpose that defines the ways in which a city may grow.

The car is our "mechanical mother-in-law." We have to maintain good relations with her, but we can't let her dominate our lives. We have to know how to coexist with the automobile without becoming its slave.

The streets are a stage and a setting too important to serve only one function, so they must acquire multiple uses over time.

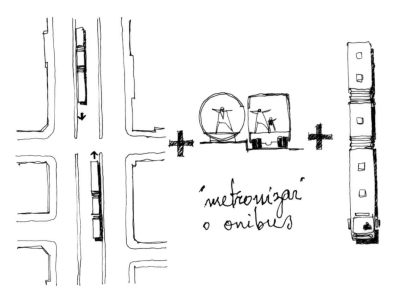

Illustration courtesy of Instituto Jaime Lerner.

CREATIVE LEISURE VS. INDUSTRIOUS MEDIOCRITY

Is it possible to do the right thing before we do the wrong thing? A hallowed principle says that industrious mediocrity sometimes wins out over idle creativity. For those who do not constantly question their own actions, it's always easier to carry out someone else's ideas.

Bus Rapid Transit station, Curitiba. Photo by Mario R. Duran Ortiz.

Industrious mediocrity is gaining ground, along with merchants of complexity: the bean-counters and the inconclusive, never-ending researchers. But sometimes, just one stroke of creativity is acupuncture powerful enough to make progress.

When we were implanting one of the most important improvements in Curitiba's transit system, Bus Rapid Transit, stepless boarding was essential. The first battle was to get hold of a large-capacity, articulated bus. We had to convince the chassis manufacturers that it was possible to build such a thing and that there was a market for it.

Through Karlos Rischbieter, a former finance minister and ex-member of the board of Volvo, I managed to arrange a meeting with Volvo's board of directors in Göteborg, Sweden. We set up one study of the cities that needed solutions for surface travel and another to see whether this would be technically viable in Curitiba.

Imagine our surprise to find that a powerful organization like Volvo had no more than a folder of newspaper clippings about mass transportation! They were embarrassed—so embarrassed that, two months later, their vice president came to Brazil to tell me they were willing to start developing the chassis in Curitiba, online with the team in Göteborg.

When the chassis was ready, it was tested late at night to see if a bus of that length would function on our streets and on our bus-only lanes. The articulated bus was impressive—it could carry 270 passengers. It was a major victory.

But it was equally important to make fare-paying and boarding/disembarking quick and agile. So it was essential that passengers pay before getting on the bus and that boarding/disembarking be stepless, on the same level of the platform.

Payment was easily resolved with a turnstile at the entrance of the tube station. But the boarding/disembarking procedure also had to be perfect, to prevent slowdowns or bottlenecks and to avoid accidents. An impeccable connection between bus and tube was essential.

We were approached by a huge number of sellers of complex and costly solutions. One proposed solution was for the bus to dock and depart by electronic means. Every solution presented to us was extremely expensive—as expensive as the bus fleet itself.

Then the architect Carlos Ceneviva called over the bus driver who was the chief of operations, Roberto Nogari, and asked him if he could stop the bus in the tube station with the door exactly opposite the loading platform. Without hesitation, the driver stationed the bus perfectly.

Ceneviva then asked him and the other drivers if they could always repeat the same maneuver with the same precision. The driver had an immediate solution—a small mark on the bus window and another on the station. When the two lined up, the operation was done perfectly, quickly, and safely. The system has worked for eleven years without a single accident.

It was creative acupuncture and a great victory over laborious mediocrity.

Mamam by Louise Bourgeois. In front of the Guggenheim Museum, Bilbao. Photo by Vicente Villamón, Flickr. Creative Commons BY-SA 2.0.

SELF-ESTEEM IS GOOD ACUPUNCTURE

How much do you like your city? Generally, you like your city because you were born there. But what do you really think of your city? Do you know it, feel part of it? Or have the naysayers convinced you that there's no solution, and you're sure that your city has the worst infrastructure, is the most violent and unfair? And it's worse if it's a big city, where the problems are just as big and it's easy to justify your frustration by scale.

But scale has nothing to do with the fact that a proposal may be unviable, nor the lack of funds. What is important is the correct vision, and a competent set-up of a "coresponsibility equation." What's needed is a scenario, or an idea, a desirable concept. And all of the people—or most—will help bring it to fruition. It's precisely at the moment of execution that a people's self-esteem helps a city move forward.

The city of Joinville, in the state of Santa Catarina in Brazil, decided to become a center of excellence in ballet. The mayor joined a campaign by choreographer Jô Braska Negrão to create a branch school of Moscow's Bolshoi Ballet, and the entire city worked to make it happen.

Claude Nobis led a campaign to make Montreux, Switzerland, the host of one of the world's most important jazz festivals, and the whole city is reaping its benefits.

Nova Jerusalem, in the poor Brazilian state of Pernambuco, annually stages the Passion of Christ at Easter time in areas throughout the town, and the spectacle has raised the self-esteem of the city—and of all Brazilian people.

To stimulate self-esteem is fundamental acupuncture. That's what happened with urban transport and solutions for waste disposal in Curitiba. It's what happened in Bilbao with the Guggenheim Museum and all its other recent conquests.

Light reflected in the Prinsengracht Canal, Amsterdam. Photo by Jethro Morsink.

LIGHT IS GOOD ACUPUNCTURE

We've said that identity is an important part of the quality of life of a city and that to know a city is to respect it and to be part of it. Starting in 1971, Curitiba began to reinforce its highway network with public lighting. That is, the public lighting system came to highlight the basic structure of the city.

By the type and intensity of the light, you could know where you were. Yellowish sodium light (400 watts) was

Christ the Redeemer statue on Corcovado Mountain, Rio de Janeiro.
Photo by Ricardo, Flickr.

used to identify structural roadways that carried mass transportation. The feeder lines had lights of other colors, and when you reached the downtown area, the lighting also was sodium.

It became very easy to "read" the city, and it helped residents get to know it better. Unfortunately, as time went on, these "light lines" have become somewhat blurred, and the distinctions confused, but it was excellent acupuncture.

Many cities have used public lighting to perform excellent acupuncture. The Schouwburgplein in Rotterdam, the Netherlands, becomes a sprawling urban stage. Users themselves can modify the public lighting, and the nature of the square changes with lighting effects that make the space seem to float. In Amsterdam, the lights of the bridge arches are reflected in the canal waters. In fact, the entire city is reflected in the water. In the Rathausplatz, in St. Pölten, Austria, the lighting accentuates the open space of the plaza. But the most fascinating effects are in the Place des Terreaux in Lyon, France, where the light and water reflect all the surrounding façades.

But what about neon, which carries its own message on the night air? In São Paulo, in the 1970s, we proposed a neon treatment for the Vale do Anhangabaú, a downtown area and a traditional site for demonstrations, rallies and public shows. It would be neon acupuncture.

During the Rio 2000 project, we proposed creating sidewalks in the form of waves in Rio's upscale Barra da Tijuca beach district, highlighted by neon borders that would dramatically illuminate the beach and the ocean waves.

There was a time in Paris when you could personally decide what time public monuments would be lit. All you had to do was call a city desk, mark the time and place, pay a service charge, and you had your personal lighting to highlight a monument or any part of the city for someone you wanted to impress.

Nothing is more beautiful than the Christ the Redeemer statue shining atop Corcovado Mountain in Rio. The Brazilian lyrics of the song "Quiet Nights of Quiet Stars," by Antonio Carlos Jobim, say it all: "And a window looking out on Corcovado, the Redeemer so lovely."

The canals of Annecy, Italy. Photo by Edwin K. C. Lee.

AQUA-PUNCTURE

Decades ago, I saw a movie starring Jeanne Moreau and set in the French city of Annecy, and I fell in love with the place. In Annecy, the canals were part of the city's daily life, and they led to another charming setting: Taillories Lake.

The image remained so clear in my memory that years later, as I arrived in Geneva for a meeting to discuss the quality of life in Arc-et-Senans (the former royal salt works of Claude-Nicolas Ledoux, now a UNESCO World Heritage Site), I took a taxi from the airport to the city and saw a sign that read: Annecy 32 km. I made up my mind instantly. Minutes later, I was walking by the canals of Annecy, searching for the exact spot that I had engraved in my memory. I stayed for two days in a small hotel there.

I had been in Venice years earlier and was moved by the scenery, the history, and the charm of a city that is part of mankind's heritage. But Venice also draws more tourists than it can comfortably hold. Annecy is an old-fashioned, down-home Venice.

But I don't want to talk about cities where water has such a powerful presence, like Rio de Janeiro, Hong Kong, Berne, Amsterdam, Geneva and Foz do Iguaçu. I'd rather discuss cities that have used water as a tool for urban acupuncture. In other words, *aqua-puncture*.

I'll also mention the cities that have straight-jacketed their canals, covered over their rivers, created environmental disasters. Cities like Los Angeles and São Paulo have turned their backs on rivers and continue to abuse them, transforming them into flood sites and deposits of waste and garbage—an attitude of disregard toward the rivers that have marked their course in history.

But there are also cities like Seoul, which is revitalizing the Cheonggyecheon River. It's similar to the way Curitiba transformed the Iguaçu River into a clean-up project, from its springs all the way to its mouth. These rivers and canals don't have to be big. In Paris, the old Canal Saint-Martin was recuperated, reviving a symbol of the city's old bohemian years. In Freiberg, Germany, downtown areas are connected by an ancient system of small, inter-linked canals known as *bäckle*. Little more than 30 cm wide, they are a constant presence in public areas. In Lyon itself, in the Place des Terreaux, light and water perform a lovely *pas-de-deux* in a unique setting.

Duck at the Saint-Martin Canal, Paris. Photo by Nicolas Vigier, http://boklm.eu/.

I personally will never forget the revitalization of the Belém, Barigui, and Iguaçu rivers, as well as the Pedreiras Park in Curitiba. I find the interventions in these rivers remarkable because they demonstrate a different approach to dealing with urban macrodrainage, one that is *for* the city, its people, and its natural environment. Instead of channeling the rivers and burying them in concrete, they were preserved in their natural course and the riparian areas protected, creating public parks for Curitiba that at the time had a grand total of one. In the Belém and Barigui rivers, lakes were created. These lakes, which are actually flood control mechanisms, also add beautifully to the landscape of these sites.

The Pedreiras Park shows how a manmade wound in the landscape can be transformed into something positive for the city. After being exhausted as quarry sites, these areas were abandoned, creating a problem in the neighborhood. A more generous look at those carved holes in the ground revealed the striking enclosed spaces they formed, inspiring the creation of two new venues: the Pedreira Paulo Leminski, an open-air concert hall where performers such as José Carreras and Paul McCartney have been featured; and the Ópera de Arame, an ethereal glass and steel theatre against the hard rock background, built in time for the Festival de Teatro de Curitiba.

It is truly a matter of how one looks at things—either as a problem or as an opportunity to do something creative. Perhaps, if kissed by the right princess, every frog can be turned into a prince.

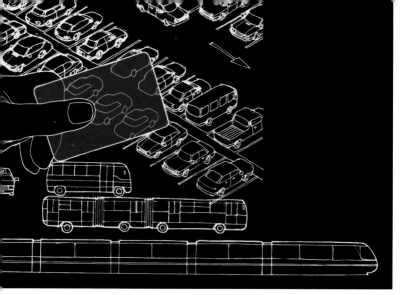

Illustration courtesy of Instituto Jaime Lerner.

THE MOBILITY CARD

Acupuncture isn't always a physical transformation. Sometimes it's simply a good idea that can change a city's life for the better. Big cities face terrible circulation problems and deterioration brought on by excessive concern with the automobile.

Even cities that responded to this nefarious tendency and made public transportation the priority, reducing excessive use of the automobile, still face these problems. The compulsion to extend the reach of automobiles into ever more densely populated areas persists.

Cities like Paris and London, which have extensive metro networks and quality systems of surface transportation, still have a high percentage of automobile use. What to do with that part of the population that insists on using cars?

London took the first radical step, charging a toll for cars entering the downtown area, and I believe the idea of reducing car access to city centers will be widely repeated.

I have nothing against the automobile. But the idea is to use it correctly and adequately, not allow it to make the city center unviable. I think the best solution is the creation of a mobility card.

The pre-paid card can be used for all travel inside the city. Starting with perimeter parking, where you leave your car and take the metro or the bus, all is paid for with the same card. You can even use it for taxis.

The solution for more rational mobility is the integration of all means of transportation. The secret is not to allow cars, taxis, buses, surface transport systems, and subways to compete on the same itinerary. The mobility card, by demanding fast integration in order for it to work properly, will allow everyone to own a BMW—Bus, Metro, or Walking.

$$sustainability = \frac{saving}{wasting}$$

ECO-CLOCK

This is another idea that doesn't require physical transformation, but rather solidarity with your neighbor and with future generations. Many have tried to motivate people around the world with the concept of sustainable development. But the explanations are confusing—either too academic or too political—and there's no comprehension in them, just enthusiasm.

People often think they can't do anything, and are quick to join the naysayers. The media don't help because they also make catastrophic predictions, as if things never change. But how can we change if people don't know what to do?

Look, it's so easy. If you want to change the environment, it's not enough simply to feel like a terminal patient.

Start with two simple things: Separate your organic waste from what's recyclable and use your car less. You'll be conserving energy, saving trees, and helping your country become less dependent on others. Save more and waste less.

That's why I'm proposing the creation of an *eco-clock* for each home. It's a clock that keeps track of the proportion of what you spend compared to what you save. If the ratio is greater than one, you are hurting your neighbor and the environment, because you're consuming more than you save. If you don't save anything you're irresponsible, because the clock will register "infinite," the mark of irresponsibility.

If your eco-clock registers irresponsibility, punishment will be immediate. You'll lose the right to blab about the environment in the bar with your friends. And you can't be president of an NGO.

Tree-lined street in Shanghai. Photo © Son Gallery™. Courtesy of iStockphoto.com.

ARBORESCENCE

Vegetation can be good urban acupuncture. Cities that might not have great attractions in some areas change radically when they plant trees. Many cities achieve unity essentially through their intense vegetation.

Shanghai has trees planted every four meters along all its streets. They beautify the landscape, generate shade, and are key supports for the bamboo structures set out to dry clothes. These clothed bamboo figures look just like scarecrows.

Can anyone imagine what the Rio beachfront would be like without trees along its side streets? Trees are acupuncture that ease the pain caused by the absence of shade, life, color, and light.

Curitiba planted one million trees in less than two decades. It started with a gesture of true urban courtesy. The public was asked to help irrigate the small trees planted on the streets. The city government launched a campaign that proclaimed: "City Hall provides the shade and you supply the water."

In many cities, the housing projects are bland because of their uniformity and the absence of trees. When we instituted our housing programs, stressing diversification through a mixture of various income levels, the city of Curitiba planted trees on the streets and asked each resident to choose a fruit tree for his garden.

The layout of the streets did not allow the felling of a single standing tree, and roads were laid out to avoid the trees. The traditional scorched-earth policy of urban design had come to an end.

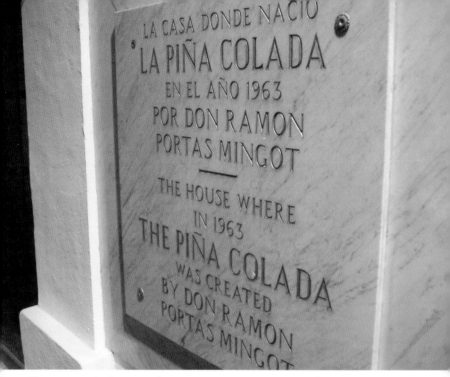

Plaque outside the Barrachina Restaurant, Puerto Rico. Photo by Bogdan Migulski, Flickr. Creative Commons BY 2.0.

PRODUCED MEMORY

Aloísio Magalhães, a pioneer of modern design in Brazil, said, "History is like a slingshot. The deeper you pull back, the farther you shoot forward."

Identity, self-esteem, the feeling of belonging—everything is related to the reference points a person has in relation to his city.

I never got tired of saying that my street in Curitiba had everything. I'd go for a walk and check the time on the train station tower. When I couldn't see it, the factory whistle next to my house told me the time. Or I knew by the smell of the Railway Workers Café, where I'd get my coffee after a night of reading or studying. There, in the station square, was a canvas airplane that photographers used as a backdrop for pictures of children.

There was the smell of the tobacco shop where I bought my comic books, the network of streetcar tracks. To this day, I can imitate the sound the train cars made arriving in the yard. I remember the smell of the varnish of the furniture polishers out front. The sounds of the irons at the tailor shop next door. The newspaper teletypes across the street, or the circus shows nearby. The fancy hotel, the radio stations, the City Hall building, the orchestras at the Curitibano Club.

All this may seem like nostalgia, but it never fades. And when it doesn't exist anymore? Do we make it up? No. We trace it back. We look to our history and culture for something that will revive or leverage various moments. Memory acupuncture?

San Francisco did this, telling the story of the places described in the books of Dashiell Hammett or the films of

Humphrey Bogart. It's the memory of fiction.

Rio de Janeiro did it, too, with the stories of the bossa nova, Bottles Alley, Nascimento Silva Street, the little bars.

The artists and performers of any age always help, singing and writing about the specific locations. People will assemble it all later, laying the groundwork for new stories.

In San Juan, Puerto Rico, a sign marks the spot where the first piña colada was made. In Hemingway's Paris, the Ritz will always be as important as any of the city monuments.

Tuileries Garden, Paris. Photo © Kiev.Victor. Courtesy of Shutterstock.com.

OF PARKS, SQUARES, AND MONUMENTS

You go to a square, but you lose yourself in a park. A square often is where you watch the world go by; a park is where you discover what lies within yourself.

Okay, it's not quite that simple. Squares and parks are like paintings: a lot depends on the frame. It's important to know which one to use.

Even more difficult is the *passe-partout*, a picture mounting with colored tape as a frame. Some squares need a small frame, and a large passe-partout. And some parks sprawl across the city, without a frame or passe-partout...such an appropriate word.

A square must have entrances. They are open to all, but with portals, they seem more special to the individual. They are small, and still can belong to millions. Sometimes, they're so big that they seem to belong to no one at all. It doesn't matter if they're closed, open, fenced-in, covered—what characterizes them all is the feeling of belonging.

There's no question that the Place des Vosges in Paris belongs to the magnificent housing that surrounds it. At the same time, it belongs to everyone. Gramercy Park in New York, surrounded by buildings, has an intimate connection with the entrances of all the structures. The sheltered plazas of New York's buildings belong to millions. They are small, but they enclose distinguished spaces.

Whether located in a vast ensemble on the outskirts of Paris or a housing project in Brazil, these large squares give us the sense that they belong to no one. But the small Italian plazas let us join them, and immediately become part of our memory. One of the smallest squares in the world, the Place de Fursten-berg in Paris, gives you the sense that it belongs just to you.

What can we say of parks? Immense, vibrant, bustling parks like Golden Gate Park in San Francisco, full of conveniences and attractions? Or those that serve as a setting for natural beauty, like the sprawling Aterro do Flamengo in Rio de Janeiro, or the French parks that create a framework and perspective for monuments, like the Tuilleries? What about those that are framed by the buildings that surround them, like Central Park in New York? Or the parks that welcome everyone, like the English parks, or those defined by veritable cathedrals of trees, like the Botanical Gardens in Rio, or massive candelabras, like the araucária pines in Barigui Park in Curitiba?

And I love the small patios typical of the small French hotels, like the patio of the Hôtel de l'Abbaye or the Relais Christine in Paris. The Spanish patios, with their fountains that drip minutes, or Pelourinho square in Salvador, with its vibrant color and smells.

I don't like the monuments of people that have no warmth or affection, or who consider themselves above the common people, with phrases intended to defend them.

I believe in a good acupuncture of sentiment, like the idea of the famous American urban designer Allan Jacobs who proposed a street lined with statues where anyone could pay homage to friends and relatives. That way, you can spend pleasant hours right now with future monuments.

And let's not forget sculptures and busts, which are also important. In Curitiba, the Polish community wished to pay the city back for creating the Papal Park in honor of the visit of John Paul II to the Paraná state capital. They decided to order a sculpture of the pope from an assistant of the renowned sculptor Pietro Bardi.

And on an important date, there we were, the governor and I as mayor, ready for the inauguration. The band was playing. An immense panel concealed the statue, which until that moment had not been revealed.

The band heightened the suspense and, with a drum roll, the panel was lifted and the pope's statue appeared. It was hideous. The pope looked like the devil from some Afro-Brazilian cult, with gleaming eyes of synthetic resin.

Pandemonium broke out.

Not even the band's futile efforts could help. An elderly Polish woman, followed by a rabid mob, brandished her parasol like a bayonet, ready to finish off whoever was responsible for the monstrosity.

The ensuing conflict and conciliation with the Polish community had some tense moments. It reminded me of a United Nations assembly. A commission came to ask me to remove the statue, which I refused to do. How could I censor a work of art?

After a few weeks, I finally reached a solution worthy of Solomon. We would try to use vegetation to cover the statue, and the Polish community would give us a high-relief image that would be permanently placed on an outdoor panel taking care that the image this time was a good likeness of the pope.

It seemed like the problem was solved. The statue would be camouflaged and the high-relief image to honor the pope's visit would be put in place—if only a supposed miracle hadn't occurred at the statue. News of the miracle spread, and people only wanted the statue's blessings. The surrogate image is still there, completely forgotten. Statues and monuments are good acupuncture when they become a part of the city's story, belonging to everyone—even if this takes a miracle.

Photo courtesy of Instituto Jaime Lerner.

THE ONE-PAGE GUIDE

Over the years, I developed the habit of making a one-page guide for each city, on every trip. The goal was to avoid wasting time. In the few days I was there in a city, I wanted to fiind out what there was to see, what was new, what was worthwhile. Sometimes, in two or three days in New York or Paris, I'd waste a lot of time just getting informed.

In this guide, I'd draw the map of the city on one side of the paper—or rather, the way I understood the city. On the other side, I'd write my agenda, with hotels, restaurants, the times and places of exhibitions, and other things that I had to see, like concerts or shows.

Soon a few friends began to ask to borrow my guide. When they came back from their trips, they'd return the copy, adding on the new things they'd discovered. And so the guide was constantly updated.

And let's not forget about the children. They also deserve their own one-page guide. It could be the cover of a school notebook, where children have a map of the city—and what's more important: they would get to know it. On the other side of the guide, children could list what they like most about the city, and exchange information with their classmates. Or maybe a state map in high-relief, a small model that would help them understand their state, its main rivers and geographic contours. This guide would be more useful than learning what the greatest common denominator is good for. I still haven't found an explanation for that.

Bicyclists and cars, Barcelona. Photo by UGT Catalunya.

URBAN CHOLESTEROL

What's the best acupuncture for high urban cholesterol? Well, first let's explain what this disease is. Urban cholesterol is the buildup of excessive automobile use in our veins and arteries. This affects people's bodies and even their minds. They soon start to think that cars are the solution for everything. So they prepare the city to revolve around the automobile. Viaducts, expressways…and fuel emissions.

The solution: Use them less. Avoid automobile use when there's a good public transportation alternative to get to where you're going.

That's good cholesterol.

But planning a city around the automobile presents another problem. The shopping center on the city's outskirts encourages us to skip exercise, to avoid a walk around town.

Separating the functions of city life—live here, work there, and take your leisure someplace else—is a waste of energy. The result is more pressure from traffic jams, wasted time, pollution, and stress.

And how many times have you denied your children an area to play in just to guarantee parking space for two cars?

Good cholesterol is controlled use of the car. And good acupuncture is throwing the keys away for a few hours.

St. Pancras Station, London. Photo by Daniel Loshak.

BUILDINGS WITH DIGNITY

The sense of belonging. That's the feeling that noble, older buildings give us when we see them on the street. They belong to the street.

They open on to the street with grandeur. And they open to their residents with generosity. Magnificent foyers,

Chrysler Building, New York City. Photo © David Pedre, courtesy of iStockphoto.com.

doors, portals, lobbies. They leave no one unsheltered, they seem to wish to give us sanctuary.

They are very unlike modern buildings, which hide their entrances or push them to the side, as if they consider these relationships secondary.

Another sensation an older building imparts is a contemplation of eternity. As if someone up there were watching.

And the crown of the building is important. It has links to the street and to immortality. It's as if the crown of a building were a form of reverence for future generations.

Modern buildings aren't like that. They simply stop, with strange structures added on, like water repositories, TV antennas and elevator shafts, exhibiting their entrails. At best, a well-groomed penthouse, or a new floor, a pool for the benefit of the privileged. They have no sense of community—of belonging—that the grand old buildings had. For this reason, I feel that the older buildings of various eras offer a form of reverence for the city. A Chrysler Building, a Crowne Building, a British train station—all have this type of commitment.

What is the commitment of a modern building? To deny us an entrance, to hide its public face, to open itself only to a select few. Surrounded by its entrails or its egoism. Its transience makes it a candidate for human demolition, because it is unperturbed by its reduction to rubble.

Musician on a quiet street, Barcelona. Photo by Alan Levine, Flickr.

ACUPUNCTURE OF SILENCE

Cities have their own sounds. In many, it's hard to hear the natural sound of the city because there's a sonic invasion of noises that mix with the sound of the city. That's a shame, because its natural sound is part of the city's identity.

I had a marvelous experience in Ferrara, Italy. It's a city that convinces me that a silence is possible that will allow us to hear the sounds of the city. It's not an absolute silence, but the absence of the distortion of the natural urban sounds.

You hear conversations; you hear the sounds of the urban environment. All this simply heightens the beauty of Ferrara, a traditional, historic city with one of the oldest universities in Europe. Ferrara has many young people and some very lively areas, but you can still hear the city. The sounds are real, not mixed or distorted—the unadorned sounds of a living city. Ferrara's sounds are in pure form.

The sound of a city has nothing to do with its scale or with the absence of noise. Barcelona is a noisy city, but that is its own sound in pure form, as natural as a matador's promenade. The sound of the avenues, the conversations, are part of the city's identity. In noisy Barcelona, there is also a silence that allows us to hear the sound if the city.

Ferrara and Barcelona speak to us of normal days. It's the sound that makes up the day-to-day life of the city. But there are cities that on certain days—special days—also have special sounds. To hear the sound of these cities, on these days, is a magical moment.

On Yom Kippur in Jerusalem, you can hear the sound of this magic moment. Little by little, the city grows quiet, the noise falls to a hush, there are no more sounds, just whispers.

The cars stop. There aren't just a few cars, like on a weekend or holiday—there are none! Not a single car. The streets are empty as grown-ups and children walk quietly along the vehicle paths. The cars are all parked, as if they had been abandoned. There's no sound of trucks, buses, pickups, motors—nothing, absolutely nothing motorized on the streets.

There's a deep, low murmur in the city, and people walk silently in sneakers or sandals—nothing that makes noise. There seems to be a collective desire to walk through the streets, with no fear of its former tenants. The conversations produce a kind of murmur—a holy whisper.

On the Day of Atonement, everything comes to a standstill in Jerusalem. In other cities there is some minor activity, but in Jerusalem everything simply stops. It's a law that all respect, whether they are religious or not. The elderly, young people, and children walk to the synagogues carrying books, while others wear their *tallithim* right on the street.

Groups of young people sit on the street and talk. The crowd leaving the synagogue fills the streets, and the conversations go on for hours and hours. Setting aside the religious aspect, you suddenly realize that it's simply a tremendous chitchat.

Streets without cars make me wonder if a global "strike" is possible—a pact among city dwellers all over the world to discover how much better their cities would be without cars. To learn how silence is important for the quality of life, or simply to isolate the sounds of the city.

As Yom Kippur ends, people wait for the first star to come out. They walk toward the huge open-air patio at the Wailing Wall to await the call of the *shofar*. Trumpets that once brought the walls tumbling down now sound for a people who anchor their identity in this wall, a few stones that have been a reference for thousands of years

In Istanbul, there's a magic moment every day. Late in the afternoon, as Muslims begin their evening prayers, there's a sudden silence. Silence allows for only the sound of the city to be heard at this special hour.

The transformation is instant—and amazing. A bustling, dynamic metropolis of nearly 10 million people suddenly falls silent. A voice echoes in succession from all the minarets of the city. At this exact moment, the sound of the city is the voice of faith.

Good acupuncture of silence is allowing the natural sound of cities to be heard. Silence that purifies, that tunes in the city's true sound. In the old days, lamplighters had the noble mission of lighting the gas lamps that illuminated the city's streets. In a similar way, my dream was to be a tuner of cities, highlighting their true sound.

Galleria Vittorio Emanuele, Milan. Photo by Sanket Agrawal.

RAMBLAS AND GALLERIES

Can the simple layout of a street influence a city's behavior? The acupuncture performed by the *ramblas* of Barcelona, the routes that link the city's central plaza to its historic port, seems to say yes.

Barcelona is one of the most exciting and spirited cities in the world, or perhaps the most vibrant. You can't credit only the Catalan spirit for this energy. It is a sum of factors.

Barcelona is one of the most densely populated cities in the world, infused with the Catalan spirit, the Mediterranean, its history and background. Yet the design of the rambla is the ideal setting for urban life. Through its ample pedestrian space and diverse surroundings, it acts as a catalyst for unique interactions and experiences. In the early hours of the morning, it's already percolating. And the fiesta that unfolds during the day makes it an ideal meeting place. People are both actors and spectators of the pageant that is Barcelona. Sure, other cities also have musicians, mimes, and magicians on their streets. But none of them sees the pageant unfold so frequently.

It's almost like a movie—each section of the rambla is a bazaar unto itself.

Every city has galleries. Some are simple, just stores side-by-side, while others are grandiose, like the Vittorio Emanuele gallery in Milan. It's the most beautiful meeting place in the city. Or like the GUM shops in Moscow, or the Lafayette Gallery—actually a department store—in Paris.

But the city with the greatest number and the widest variety of galleries, without a doubt, is Paris. The Vivienne and Colbert galleries, interconnected, are magnificent. So is the Passage des Panoramas, near the Bourse. What delights me in these galleries isn't only that they are ancient covered

GUM department store, Moscow. Photo by Andrew Anderson.

Street performers in Güell Park, Barcelona. Photo by David Ellis.

passages. It's the quality of the stores, the shop windows, and the attention to detail. And, of course, their ability to sell lace, ribbons, cake decorations, and music boxes with the dignity of a merchant offering the world's most price-less treasures.

But the biggest weapon—real heavy artillery—is in the galleries of the Palais Royal plaza: the armies of toy soldiers on display. You can even buy medals at these stores, and walk out more decorated than a field marshal on parade.

Interior of the Ópera de Arame, Curitiba. Photo by Herval Freire.

A PINPRICK DOESN'T HURT

In acupuncture, the prick of the needle has to be quick.

You can't imagine acupuncture with the needles being inserted slowly and painfully. Acupuncture requires speed and precision.

The same applies to urban acupuncture. That was how we implanted the first pedestrian zone in Curitiba, in 1972. The whole operation took just 72 hours.

I still remember the loud protest of shop owners when we announced the project. We knew the idea would be hard to implement, because work could be stopped by a court order in favor of a protest. We had to work fast—very fast. My public works secretary predicted it would take a few months, at least. I insisted on speed and set a deadline of 48 hours. I'm sure they thought I was crazy. Then the secretary came and told me it would be possible to finish in a month. Once again, I refused. And more new proposals were presented for the project's execution: to prepare the street furniture beforehand; to mobilize special teams to prepare the new pavement in each block.

The time kept shrinking until the secretary reached his limit: one week. I contested it and managed to reach an agreement on a period of 72 hours. We'd start on a Friday night and present the finished work to the public the next Monday night.

If the people didn't approve the change, we could always go back to what we had before. But it was essential that the people see the finished work. And that's what we did.

A day after the inauguration, one of the businessmen who had headed a petition opposing the project made another request: that the work continue to expand and include more regions.

The Ópera de Arame theatre, erected on the site of an abandoned quarry, was concluded in sixty days. The idea wasn't to break records, but some public works, for special reasons, need to be done quickly. With the Ópera de Arame, we didn't want to miss the chance to host an International Theater Festival. A political dispute between the governor and the sponsors led him to prohibit holding the festival in the Guaíra Theater, the city's main arena. So the need arose to build the Ópera de Arame in time to host the festival. We started on January 15.

Two months later, on March 18, we inaugurated the theater. To finish the project in such a short time, we used only one type of material, steel tubes. We held only one bidding for labor. It was an odyssey.

Another project executed extremely quickly was Passaúna Park, which had to be finished before a new government took office. The governor at the time also was politically opposed, but he understood the need to protect river springs. We built a park in twenty-eight days, even before a topographical study. Everything was decided and carried out right at the work site. The Open University of the Environment was completed in two months, also a record.

More recently, the NovoMuseu, or the Oscar Niemeyer Museum, was built in just five months. You can imagine how complex a project like that is, but we had a chance to recycle an old building designed by Oscar Niemeyer himself: a magnificent, audacious project of the 1960s that was transformed into offices for the state secretaries. It was important to transform a bureaucratic area into a space dedicated to creativity, identity, art, design, architecture, and cities. Once again, speed was of the essence.

And the museum is there to this day, embodying the genius of Oscar Niemeyer in a project whose cost—$12 million—is far less than the outlay for a branch of the Guggenheim.

The speed of these acupunctures had a single goal: to prevent the inertia of complex vendors, of pettiness, of bad politics, from making these critical moments and fundamental projects unviable.

Festival of Lights at Brandenburg Gate, Berlin. Photo © AR Pictures. Courtesy of Shutterstock.com.

TROMPE L'OEIL

Sometimes the city resorts to something false to preserve what is true. That's the case with the panels at a work site that show what a building will look like after restoration.

It's what happened with the restoration of the Madeleine in Paris. Panels screening the work site showed a Madeleine even more beautiful than the original.

Another fantastic example of *trompe l'oeil*—French for "trick the eye"—is the illusionist decoration of the nave and the dome of the Church of Gesù in Rome, which were added on a century later. Or the Church of Santo Inácio de Loyola, where the cupola, projected but not built, was veiled by a trompe l'oeil in a false perspective.

In Berlin, during the reform of the Brandenburg Gate, giant panels were installed to conceal the work. Images of the city were placed on them to create a different perspective.

A trompe l'oeil that doesn't help the city is a shopping mall, with the same stores, the same logos, so that you can't even tell what city you're in. That's really a trompe l'oeil that brings no benefits.

But a good store window can be a lovely trompe l'oeil. I don't know of any city that has lovelier store windows than Paris. It's like watching a parade of colors.

Everything has its own display, from the simplest hotel to the most sophisticated stores. It's a sightseeing tour created by people eager to show you their best side. Maybe this image of the city is false—or at least incomplete—but it can be valuable nonetheless. Maintaining pride and self-esteem requires continuous acupuncture.

Many resort to the trompe l'oeil for shock effect, to create a false perspective or accentuate the absurd. This is an old issue that reminds me of the discussion between True and False:

False told True: "I got here first."

Shop window, Paris. Photo by Beatriz Sirvent Valera.

True replied: "You barely exist, and I am the end-all."

"Without me," said False, "you wouldn't be true. You, by yourself, could be false or true. When we're together, I—because I'm false—will lie and be truly whole. And you, with your truth, could be considered false."

In this case, acupuncture consists of making the false work on behalf of the true.

Federico Fellini directing, 1972. © John Springer Collection/CORBIS.

A LETTER TO FELLINI

We lived in the heyday of the Italian cinema. Fellini, Ettore Scola, Pasolini, Visconti, and so many other magical directors. And at one point, the city of Curitiba wrote a letter to Fellini. The story goes something like this:

We got news that Federico Fellini would come to Brazil for the Biennial of Arts in São Paulo. A popular movement arose in Curitiba to convince Fellini to visit the city. The idea was to pay tribute to the recently deceased composer Nino Rotta—composer of the soundtracks for most of Fellini's films—by naming an auditorium after Rotta, an auditorium to be built in a quarry that I, as mayor, had deactivated.

We decided to invite Fellini to inaugurate the Nino Rotta auditorium. But how to make the invitation?

Journalists Aramis Milarch and Valêncio Xavier and a large number of Curitiba's filmmakers and movie buffs felt that the invitation should be made in the form of a movie. The invitation would be presented by Fellini-esque characters in various parts of the city. In other words, Curitiba would be described to Fellini in his own language.

The next days were filled with intense creativity. The film was finished. The final scene took place in the quarry itself, with Italian painter Franco Giglio giving a *pernacchia* to movie directors (or, in English, "blowing a raspberry").

Who should deliver the letter? We thought of Giglio himself, who supposedly was a friend of Fellini. But by this time, it had been so much fun making the film that we had all but forgotten Fellini.

However, the mission demanded that we keep going. And so our own Franco Giglio went with his wife Rose to the Dolce Aqua, in compliance with a personal appeal from his family. But Franco Giglio was so shy that he never managed to deliver the film-invitation. Years later, Giglio died without ever having completed his task.

Nonetheless, the great auditorium was built in the quarry and, next to it, in another quarry, we erected the Ópera de Arame theatre.

I don't think Fellini ever knew that the desire to honor him had created such lovely acupuncture.

Oh yes, and the film *Letter to Fellini* won prizes at various film festivals.

Statue of Hachiko, Tokyo. Photo by Dominiek ter Heide, Flickr. Creative Commons BY 2.0.

HOW TO FIND SOMEONE IN A CITY

A city should allow people not only to meet, but also to be found.

Finding someone in Caracas, Venezuela, outside its best-known landmarks, is hard enough. Urban references aren't of much help.

In Tokyo, it's much harder. There are private codes that each city creates, with indications that only residents understand.

And how do you find someone in Dolce Acqua, Italy? Once, my wife Fani and I disembarked in Nice. We passed through Monte Carlo and, on the road, we remembered that we were near San Remo, where our Italian *pintore* Franco Giglio lived.

At a gas station, I learned that eight kilometers north of Ventimiglia there was a place called Dolce Acqua, near the ruins of a castle, next to the Nervia River.

We had the feeling that all we had to do was shout "Franco Giglio" and we'd find him. Just go yelling through the streets, "Franco, Franco Giglio!"

A few minutes later, we were in front of a medieval stone bridge. When we got across, we gave the first shout: "Franco, Franco Giglio!" A boy came running up: "Il pintore brasiliano? He's at Pastio's bar."

Inside the bar, we found a fog of tobacco smoke and the agreeable sound of men drinking and talking. We gave our second shout: "Franco, Franco Giglio!"

One of the men took us by the hand and led us to a two-storey house. "Franco, Franco Giglio!" And he opened the window.

With three shouts, you can still find someone in a good city.

But few meeting spots could have a more beautiful story than that of Hachiko, in Tokyo. Hachiko was an Akita, a breed of dog native to Japan, and in the 1920s had belonged to a professor at the University of Tokyo, formerly the Imperial University. Everyday, Hachiko would follow Professor Eizaburo Ueno to the Shibuya station where he would take the train to work. Each day at 3:00 p.m., Hachiko would go back to the station to wait for his owner's return.

On May 21, 1925, Professor Ueno had a stroke and died at the university. For nearly nine years after that, Hachiko kept going back to the station every afternoon to wait for his friend who would never return. On March 7, 1934, Hachiko died in the same spot where he always waited for the professor.

The story of Hachiko was already famous in the city, and one month after the dog died, a statue was placed at the entrance of the Shibuya station in his honor. The bronze statue, ninety-one centimeters high, was made by the artist Teru Ando. During the Second World War, all the statues were confiscated and melted down to make weapons, including the statue of Hachiko. In 1948, Takeshi Ando, the son of the original sculptor, was hired to make a replica, which was placed in the same spot as before. The original Hachiko was stuffed and placed on exhibit in the Museum of Natural Sciences in Tokyo.

Hachiko's life was recounted in a book and in a movie entitled *The Story of Hachiko*. Visitors passing through the Shibuya station can buy presents or memorabilia of the city's favorite dog in the Shibuya No Shippo store. A colored mosaic depicting Akitas covers a wall near the station.

March 7 came to be the date when the Hachiko Festival was celebrated, in honor of canine loyalty. The statue of Hachiko has become a prime meeting spot in Tokyo. At any hour of the day, someone is there with his eye on the clock, waiting for a friend.

Niterói Contemporary Art Museum, Rio de Janeiro. Photo by Rodrigo Soldon, Flickr. Creative Commons BY-ND 2.0.

THE PRESENCE OF GENIUS

The presence of genius has clearly marked the history of many important cities around the world.

It's impossible to count how often this happened in Italian cities, the home of Renaissance masters such as Michelangelo, Da Vinci, Titian, and Botticelli.

But none of them feels the presence of genius like Barcelona. There aren't many works by Gaudí in the city—

Güell Park, the Mila House, La Sagrada Família cathedral, the Batlló House, the Vicens House. Nevertheless, Barcelona breathes Gaudí. He seems to be everywhere, even in works he had nothing to do with. Still, my favorite genius in Barcelona is the architect Lluís Domènech i Montaner, designer of the Palau de la Música Catalana, among others.

In Rio, Oscar Niemeyer doesn't have many works—there's the Obra do Berço, the Ministry of Education building, the Museum of Contemporary Art in Niterói across the bay. But Rio is Oscar Niemeyer. Just as it's also Millôr, Vinicius de Moraes, Antonio Carlos Jobim, Cartola, and Burle Marx.

The city of Belo Horizonte has even more works by Niemeyer, including the Pampulha project, amongst others. But still, the soul of the city is Milton Nascimento.

Caratinga, another city in the state of Minas Gerais, is Ziraldo.

Curitiba is Poty. Porto Alegre is Mário Quintana. Bahia is Dorival Caymmi, Gilberto Gil and Caetano Veloso.

You can try to rationalize any city, but genius is essential.

Cities need everything, but it's good to know genius also is required.

Front gate of La Boqueria market, Barcelona. © Ingenui. Courtesty of iStockphoto.com.`

MARKETS AND STREET FAIRS

Why does a market attract so many people? There are many explanations: people like to watch people; the market is as old as the city itself; people like to see other people doing the same thing they are; and people like to see food, its preparation, its care.

With the modernization of cities and globalization, we began to receive and buy things that were overly packaged, exceedingly ready to use, in places that were too perfectly prepared. We don't see things in their raw state, their original form. That's why we feel nostalgic when we see products, fruits, vegetables, meats, and fish in their natural state.

The modern zoo will no longer be a place for lions, giraffes, jaguars, and pelicans, but rather an area for chickens, cows, pigs, ducks, and sheep.

Why is the La Boqueria market in Barcelona one of the best in the world? Because it's gorgeous, with its stained glass windows, and because the way its products are presented is also attractive. The meats, the fruits, and green vegetables all smell fresh, and the whole atmosphere affects the vendors, who are lively and cheerful. It's great to feel this early in the morning. Breakfast in a café inside the market is unforgettable.

We all get tired when we see everything the same. A regular shopping mall excludes us from the city, with its stores so identical that it's hard to know what city you're in. But the markets and street fairs have always been a reference point for a city.

Paris was the ultimate loser when they demolished the Les Halles market designed by Victor Balthard. Nothing could ever replace the buoyant life of the "underbelly of Paris."

But we don't have to leave Brazil to find iconic marketplaces. The São Paulo Market is an important one.

The Grand Bazaar, Istanbul. Photo by Stephen Downes, www.downes.ca.

And it will be even better after the São Pedro Park is restored and revitalized as planned. The Curitiba Municipal Market doesn't have the same tradition, but it's still a good market. The nostalgia that immigrants from poor northeastern Brazil feel for their home was precisely what made their typical market in Rio as attractive as any in the Northeast.

In Amsterdam, the Albert Cuyp Markt, every Monday morning, and the Noorder Markt and the Waterlooplein in the Jewish quarter, are as good as any in Europe. The Feskekôrka, in Göteborg, Sweden, is a spectacular market, even though it can't compare to the Great Bazaar of Istanbul or the Spice Bazaar, with their special, singular traits.

And what can anyone say about the Tokyo fish market? In this immense terrestrial sea of fish and octopi, we feel like scuba divers without tanks.

Still, nothing transcends the richness, the sheer pleasure of haggling and negotiating in an Arabian *souk*. Normally, the alleys are very narrow, and the merchants sit outside the shops. With the little space that's left, you're forced to look from one side to the other. The merchant has already gotten what he wanted: your attention. You're already lost, and you'll end up buying. So now, do as they do—make this your pleasure. It is here, deep in the cities and Arab quarters, that commerce brings us the flavor of identity.

Time, always adding new layers to civilization, is nostalgic for the primitive state of things that allows us to come, conclude, and achieve something.

That's why the most sophisticated styles and trends seek the most rustic, least developed settings to stand out and be photographed.

Man seeks his neighbor in the market, doing the exact same thing in bustling locations.

The marketplace is acupuncture of identity at a time when many cities are losing theirs.

Counter at The Dagda, a pub in Edinburgh, Scotland. Photo by Joe Gordon.

THE BAR COUNTER

Support, a sense of comfort, an alert mind—all are reflections of good acupuncture.

That's why a good bar counter is important. The Spanish like to say that a good *barra* is what's important.

A counter is important anytime, anywhere in the world. From the old emporium, where you would buy household supplies and stop at the counter for a good chat and an antipasti before heading home, to the sophisticated bars and happy hours of the big cities.

Small, big, round—the single most important thing, besides the product itself, the food or drink, is the tolerance and understanding of the barman. From the *champanerias* of Barcelona to the Irish pubs of New York, or the simple taverns of Rio, all must have this feeling of solidarity. The patience to hear the same old stories, that no one in your own house can stand to hear any longer.

Which is the best counter? A Rio tavern has the informality, the complicity, and the feeling of celebration. Celebrating what? I don't know—maybe celebrating the friendship of someone you don't know well enough to recognize his flaws.

I remember the counter of P.J. Clark's in New York City, which is—or was—designed to help you hold on to the handrail and balance on the barstool. Or the cafeteria counters in New York, where the early-morning conversations start up against a backdrop of griddles and spatulas preparing eggs in every conceivable style, while Latinos on one side and Americans on the other engage in a morning *salsa*. Sometime ago, I headed across Central Park to a cafeteria in the Excelsior Hotel just to see how fast a 70-year-old man could wait on his clients from around the neighborhood. I don't know if he's still there, but it was a cafeteria counter operating at lightning speed.

By the way, speed at the counter is essential. The *barra* of a tavern in Bilbao or San Sebastian has a double line of waiters and a triple line of clients. Ham and red wine, blood sausage, clams, eels, all come forth with noise and efficiency.

amazon.com

SDR2RYGpMk

Your order of March 17, 2015 (Order ID 104-9153287-9773843)

Qty.	Item	Item Price	Total
4	Urban Acupuncture Lerner, Jaime --- Hardcover (°° 1-A-7 °°) 1610915836	$17.22	$68.88

This shipment completes your order.

Have feedback on how we
packaged your order? Tell us at
www.amazon.com/packaging.

Subtotal	$68.88
Shipping & Handling	$6.96
Promotional Certificate	$-6.96
Tax Collected	$6.00
Order Total	$74.88
Paid via credit/debit	$74.88
Balance due	$0.00

V4

Returns Are Easy! Most items can be refunded, exchanged, or replaced when returned
in original and unopened condition. Visit http://www.amazon.com/returns to start your
return, or http://www.amazon.com/help for more information on return policies.

7/DR2RYGpMk/-4 of 4-/-/BF5/sss-us/4285238/0322-12:30/0317-16:42

In Berlin, at the Gendarmenmarkt, a counter on wheels stretches to the sidewalk so the talk can continue outside. It's a convertible counter, like a sports car.

At the *sushi-yas* of Tokyo, the plates of sushi slide along a belt on the counter in front of the client. On the other side of the oval or circular belt stand the sushi men, working swiftly and tirelessly. The client's only job is to follow the parade of dishes along the belt and choose the kind of sushi that most appeals to him. Afterward, all he has to do is count the dishes and pay the bill. In Tokyo, there are bars in nooks so snug that the all they have is the counter and no more than a dozen stools.

The bar's counter represents a clean start, similar to the turn at the end of a lane for a swimmer at the pool. A good turn at the counter is a dive into a fresh moment of the day when, in the words of the journalist Nireu Teixeira, "the night will be like a filter, and only the good remains."

Is it surprising that there are so many bars around a pool? The most beautiful in New York is in Williamsburg, Brooklyn, with a fake pool lit up in an old garage. I want that light designer in my city.

The English pub places great importance on the counter. Some of them even have dividing partitions, a sort of reserved area—maybe a confessional? Can you imagine a western saloon, or an advertising set, without a bar?

Bars require certain boldness in conversation, because someone has to take the initiative. For young people, they're a good place to shed their insecurity; for the lonely, a place to share their solitude.

From the barras of the *bajo-rasantes* in San Sebastian to the bar in front of the Bosphorus in Istanbul, the counter is acupuncture against solitude, and in favor of the city.

Some are special, like Box 32 at the Market in Florianopolis, a democratic space for the frequenters of the Market and as sophisticated as patrons may wish. From meat pastries to champagne.

Another very special bar counter is at Maneko's in Curitiba, which made its mark in history with the only solemn, ritual passage of bar ownership on record.

Before it became Maneko's, the bar was known as Mano's, and it was in a gallery where my barber, Ze Trindade, also worked. It was called the Gallery of Commerce, but if any place ever looked like a Bolivian metro station, this was it. The place was home to all kinds of strange activities—a doll and toy repair shop, an umbrella restorer, a penny arcade. The primary meeting spot was a place called Mano's Bar where people would sit with a view of the arcade.

On Jan. 1, 1984, Mano transferred the place to the new owner, Manoel Alves, in the presence of customers and friends, with the promise that the cook Ida and the waiter Nilson Passarinho would keep their jobs, and the bar would continue to offer its traditional snacks, such as codfish cakes and prepared cow hoof.

Unlike many political promises, this one was kept and is honored even today in the bar that was relocated in 1988 to Cabral Boulevard, barely 100 meters away, with the name Maneko's in honor of its new owner. Manoel Alves showed a true gesture of urban courtesy and solidarity with his clientele.

There's only one thing the bar counter sometimes produces and must be rigorously repelled: the bore. They tell me that in the Brazilian city of Poços de Caldas there was a bar owner who would ring a bell every time he felt a bore approaching. It was a warning—and such a responsibility!

There's the sophistication of the *vin* bars in Paris, where you can sample every type of wine. And there are the simple taverns of Rio, an endless source of tasty snacks, good draft beer, and a certain open bonhomie.

Ah, the bars of Rio. Nothing matches their simplicity, sympathy, and tolerance. Because the bar counter requires a good dose of tolerance from the owner toward his customers, a fundamental human trait.

And the zinc counters of the tabac cafés of Paris, where the morning begins with a *tartine*, a coffee, a glass of wine, or a *marc*. No matter. It's "La Marseillaise" saluted with glasses of Pernod.

But the solidarity of a bar is measured by the relationship between the length of the counter and the number of tables. The longer the counter, the greater the solidarity. Because the bar counter represents a state of equilibrium for each patron, a stable place to weigh their options, to reflect on the past and consider the future. It's the undercurrent, running beneath the surface.

Pont Neuf, Paris. Photo by Bruno Mariotti, Flickr. Creative Commons BY-SA 2.0.

LOVE FOR THE CITY

What if each needle prick of acupuncture were a gesture of love for your city? Begin by drawing your city. Draw your neighborhood and mark the people you know. Greet them by name. That's good acupuncture.

Shop in the markets and places where the owners and families attend to their customers. That's another nudge of love for your city. Catch the next bus and greet the bus driver, the fare collector, and your neighbors. That's a point for you. Take a walk and notice the design on the ground, the streetlights, and the itinerary. Another point for you.

Did you hear and recognize the customary sounds of the city? Did you smell the typical odors of a certain region? More points in your favor. Did you ask the owner of the store where you usually shop not to seal the storefront with roll-down steel grates at night, so people can see the merchandise in the shop windows? More points.

Do you have a circle of friends you chat with, a café or a bar that's your regular spot? Excellent. Do you have your own barber, your newsstand? Even better. Are you a regular customer of the stores and services facing along one street? More points for you. Your eco-clock is less than one. Good.

Do you remember your city the way it used to be, don't feel the need for junk food, watch a movie in a regular cinema and discuss it later at a restaurant with your friends? Congratulations! You are now a citizen, cured by urban acupuncture.

You're able to capture the special moments in the life of a city and realize that each city can be better than it is. It's up to you to become familiar with it and sense what's best about it, which is solidarity. Then you'll be able to love people of every city.

Let's all think about the city.
Me, on my part, I think of…

I think of that darling square on 53rd Street in New York,
so precious
that should be closed
(to avoid being stolen)

I think of the streets and canals of Annecy
a down-home Venice

of the herbage covering the marquee of the Hôtel de Fenice
et des Arts in Venice,
deep in autumn

of the sheltered plazas in New York,
petite and grandiose
at the same time

I think of how fast culture breeds,
pounding and hammering on the walls
of brownstones and skyscrapers

I think of the silhouette of New York
of Koblenz
of Florence
of Jerusalem

Rooftops of Bologna, Italy. Photo by Yuri Virovets.

a great city must have a silhouette

of the color of the cities
ah, the color of Bologna
of Farol da Barra in Salvador
of the gray of Rue Monfettard bleeding through
    the colors of the market
the color of the sea, seen from the terrace of Amanda's
    Bar in San Juan,
the dignity of Via dei Calzaiouli in Florence
the hazy mornings of my gray Curitiba

and walls
I think of the eternity of the walls of Jerusalem

of China
and its valleys

I think of the doors and portals
I think of the solitude of the Place de Furstenberg
A bench, a tree, and a
street lamp
and you, so congenial with the crowd
of people that you care about
and alone with the person you love

I think of the shelters, that the city should be
one great, encompassing shelter

I think of the *ombrelones* of the Campo de' Fiori
of the *art-nouveau* marquee of a building in Paris
of the Vittorio Emanuele Gallery, a veritable cathedral
    for passers-by

I think of the counters of Rio taverns
of the family grocery shops in Curitiba

I think of the bars and the street corners
of the plazas and patios of Paris
Place Dauphine
Place des Vosges
or the Plaza Mayor in Madrid

where a hand's breadth of table
is worth a handful of prose
where waiting is more agreeable
making a date with yourself
with yourself and others

to look at a river, like a river in Paris
at canals, as in Venice or Annecy
at the sea in San Juan
at the people passing in the Champs Elysées
at yourself, as you were in the Paraguas Café
in Barcelona

to linger in the bar on a bicycle path in Curitiba
in Gramercy Park
at the window of a bar facing the
Museum of Natural History in Nova York
in the plaza in Sienna
in San Marco Square
in a simple tavern in Rio do Fogo
a few miles from Natal
at twilight in the Bosque do Papa, in Curitiba
to chat at the Passeio Público park or
at the deck of Barigui Park
in Curitiba
at a brunch in the Bela Vista Café in San Francisco
at the Boca Maldita

or at the ramblas of Barcelona
at happy hour in a hotel lobby
in New York
in the cafés of Buenos Aires

to hear the New York Philharmonic
a Benny Goodman concert at the
Church of the Heavenly Rest, in New York
a lilting samba in Garibaldi Square
or at a bar in Rio
a concert at the Sainte-Chapelle
the Klezmatics right on 2nd Avenue in New York
Villa-Lobos on a boat in the Amazon rain forest
the "Despertar da Montanha" in the streets of Ouro Preto
a flute concert in the gothic district of Barcelona

I think of the pathways and the excursions

the little stroll behind the Arco do Teles, in Rio
the Passeig de Gracia in Barcelona
and the Carrer Moncada with its museums

I think of the old houses

of Steiner Street, in San Francisco
of Heidelberg
of Rio do Fogo, in Rio Grande do Norte

of Olinda

I think of the valleys of

Jerusalem
Heidelberg
Assisi
Ouro Preto
Olinda

of the passageways and galleries
of the Rue de Seine-Dauphine
of the Paris gallery in Budapest
and the bridges,
the Charles Bridge in Prague
the Pont-Neuf in Paris
the bridges of Annecy
and of course the ones in Venice

I think of the churches
of Ouro Preto and Saint Germain
of the cathedrals of Duomo in Milan
of Reims
and the Sagrada Família in Barcelona
or the small church in Zumbi, in Rio Grande do Norte

In San Francisco, in the symphony of a city

in Edinburgh, a park that covers a train track
in London, the grace of small scale
in New York you always have the feeling
that you're just starting out
An electric blender of ideas
where you are alone, in the company
of everyone else
Rome, the city where the past
is at arm's length
In short, every city should have a personality (or a melody
    that flows) that was the one chosen to present it,
    combining admiration
for the city and the person

The cities, exactly when?
Paris in the '20s and the '60s
New York today
Barcelona in the '60s or now
Rio in the '60s
Curitiba in the '70s
Natal today
Salvador in the '70s
Ouro Preto

Because the city that I think of now
will be with me forever.

Island Press | Board of Directors